So you really want to learn

Geography

Book Two

Second Edition

So you really want to learn

Geography

Book Two

Second Edition

James Dale-Adcock

Series Editor: Simon Lewis

Independent Schools
Examinations Board

www.galorepark.co.uk

GALORE PARK

Published by ISEB Publications, an imprint of Galore Park Publishing Ltd
19/21 Sayers Lane, Tenterden, Kent TN30 6BW
www.galorepark.co.uk

Typography by Typetechnique, London W1
Illustrations by Simon Tegg and Ian Douglass
Cover illustration David Robertson Photography

Printed by LEGO, SpA, Italy

ISBN: 978 1 905735 55 6

First edition published 2007, reprinted 2008, second edition published 2011

Details of other Galore Park publications are available at
www.galorepark.co.uk

ISEB Revision Guides, publications and examination papers may also be
obtained from Galore Park.

Cover image © Tom Mackie/Alamy

Acknowledgements

OS Ordnance Survey® This product includes mapping data licensed from Ordnance Survey ® reproduced by permission of Ordnance Survey on behalf of HMSO. © Crown copyright 2007. All rights reserved. Ordnance Survey Licence number 150001477. Ordnance Survey and the OS symbol are registered trademarks and Explorer and Landranger are trademarks of the Ordnance Survey, the national mapping agency of Great Britain.

The publishers are grateful for permission to use the photographs as follows:

(*T* = Top, *C* = Centre, *B* = Bottom, *L* = Left, *R* = Right.)

P3 The Photolibrary Wales/Alamy; p14 (T) Jane Hallin/Alamy; (B) Tracey Whitefoot/Alamy; p15 (T) Michael Willis/Alamy; (C) Robert Morris/Alamy; (B) Leslie Garland Picture Library/Alamy; p34 (TL) Alan Curtis/Alamy; (TR) blickwinkel/Alamy; (BL) Marc Hill; (BR) geogphotos/Alamy; p35 (TL) stephen bond/Alamy; (BL) AfriPics.com/Alamy; (R) Colin Underhill/Alamy; p43 Robert Harding Picture Library Ltd/Alamy; p47 NSIL/Dick Roberts, Visuals Unlimited/Science Photo Library; p52 Derek Croucher/Alamy; p54 Julia Gavin/Alamy; p59 Construction Photography/Alamy; p60 Asianet-Pakistan/Alamy; p70 (TL) Michael Donne/Science Photo Library (BL) John Cancalosi/Alamy; (BR) Sebastian/Alamy; p73 (L) Jerry Mason/Science Photo Library; (R) Lea Paterson/Science Photo Library; p74 Sam Ogden/Science Photo Library; p82 Maurice Crooks/Alamy; p87 University Of Dundee/Science Photo Library; p89 Andrew Fox/Alamy; p93 NOAA/Science Photo Library; p95 Florida Images/Alamy; p103 (T) Kumar Sriskandan/Alamy; (BL) Greg Balfour Evans/Alamy; (BR) Colin Underhill/Alamy; p109 (T) Pukkashots.com/ Alamy; (B) Andrew Holt/Alamy; p110 (T) Cotswolds Photo Library/Alamy; (B) Ian Dagnall/Alamy p115 (L) David J. Green/Alamy; (R) Iain Masterton; p120 (TL) Greg Balfour Evans/Alamy; (TR) Mike Robinson/Alamy; (BL) geogphotos/Alamy; (BR) Archimage/Alamy; p125 (T) Neil Cooper/Alamy; (B) mediacolor's/Alamy; p138 NASA/Alamy; p159 SHOUT/Alamy

Contents

Introduction

This textbook is written for Year 8 pupils. Ideally it should follow on from *So you really want to learn Geography Book 1*, the foundation textbook written for Year 7 pupils. Together, these form a specific Key Stage 3 course which is particularly suited for those preparing for the ISEB Common Entrance Geography syllabus.

This textbook contains extra passages within each section which will challenge and meet the demands of pupils being prepared for Common Academic Scholarship. These extra passages are clearly marked as syllabus extra/scholarship text, and are supported by the appropriately more challenging level 2 questions to be found at the end of each section. In addition, the section on bearings has been included as a useful skill but is not required for the exam. A chapter on settlement geography is also included although only mapwork elements are required in the ISEB syllabus.

Each chapter is punctuated by key words which are highlighted in **bold**. Definitions of these key words can be found in the topic glossaries at the end of each chapter. Exam tips and summaries are also included and are useful for revision purposes. These concise text boxes provide insight into what an exam marker may be looking for in an answer and sum up the key points covered in each section.

The recently revised ISEB Common Entrance and Common Academic Scholarship syllabus places a significant emphasis on learning theory and skills based on topic case studies. This approach permeates this textbook, with every opportunity taken to relate theory and skills to detailed contemporary examples. When the syllabus demands knowledge of an example, the textbook, clearly marks this case study as a syllabus example. If a case study is not required by the syllabus but is included to reinforce theory we have marked it as an extra example.

An enquiry suggestion is offered at the conclusion of each chapter, which teachers may find useful as a stimulus for extension work. At the end of each chapter, the level 1 and level 2 questions are further reinforced by a series of questions from past papers which cover all topics of the chapter and provide a useful plenary assessment.

James Dale-Adcock

Additional resources

All textbooks in the Galore Park Geography series have answer books, which can be particularly useful for parents wishing to aid pupils with their studies.

This symbol appears throughout the text to indicate where blank maps of Britain, Europe and the world would be useful for revision. These are available for download from the Galore Park website, www.galorepark.co.uk

The *Geography ISEB Revision Guide* is an invaluable companion to this series as pupils prepare for their Common Entrance exams.

The latest Common Entrance syllabus information can be found on the ISEB website www.iseb.co.uk, and supporting material can be accessed via the Galore Park website www.galorepark.co.uk

Chapter 1: Mapwork

Being able to interpret and use an Ordnance Survey (OS) map is one of the key skills you will need in order to do well in a Geography exam. By now you are probably a skilled user of OS maps at 1:25 000 and 1:50 000 scales. This chapter will help you remember and practise the skills you have already developed, and will introduce you to further skills so that you will be able to answer any question relating to the OS map that comes with the Geography paper. This chapter will revise the following:

Using an Ordnance Survey map in the field to recognise features of the landscape

- Using four figure and six figure grid references to identify features on a map.

- Determining the direction one map feature is from another and measuring the distance between map features.

- Recognising the height of places on a map and visualising what the landscape would look like if you were at ground level.

- Understanding which map symbols are commonly used and grouping features on the map into human and physical features.

In addition, this chapter will help you understand how OS maps can be used to answer questions about other topics in Geography.

1.1 Basic skills revision: grid references, distance and height on OS maps

Mapwork words used in exam questions

More than ever the OS map is being used in several sections of Geography exams. This means that you must be skilled users of OS maps and must look out for the mapwork words used in questions relating to the map, highlighted in bold below.

You will definitely be asked questions concerning the location of map features using a **four figure grid reference** or a **six figure grid reference**. If you do not know the map symbol that appears at the grid reference given, look at the **key**, or legend, which is a list of all the different symbols on the map and the meaning of these symbols (see Appendix 1, pages 176–179). Have a look at these now.

OS maps are divided up into even squares, called **grid squares**. Whatever the scale of the OS map, the area of land covered within 1 grid square is always 1 km². Grid squares are created by the vertical and horizontal thin blue lines on the map (see Fig. 1.1.1). The vertical thin blue lines are called **eastings** because the numbers increase in value as you go east. The horizontal thin blue lines are called **northings** because the numbers increase in value as you go north. Each easting and northing is given a two digit number to be identified by and this number can be found at either end of the line.

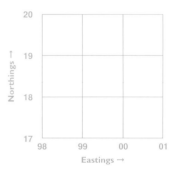

Fig. 1.1.1: Grid squares

Often a mapwork question will ask candidates to describe an aspect of the map (such as the **relief**) above or below a northing, or to one side of an easting. If you are asked to describe the relief of any given area of the map, you should describe the height of the land. You will need to use **contour lines** and **spot heights** to identify the exact height and shape of the land. Here is an example which refers to the map of Arundel on page 28:

Question: Describe the relief of the land to the north of northing 07

You might already have the mapwork skills to answer this question; if in doubt, read through the rest of this revision chapter to help you.

Using four figure grid references

In most exams you will, at least once, have to give or interpret a four figure grid reference. Four figure grid references allow you to identify a specific grid square using the numbers at either end of the eastings and northings.

Here is a reminder of what to do when you want to tell somebody where something is on a map. Remember the bottom left hand corner is the meeting point of easting and northing, whether you are giving or receiving a four figure grid reference. Use the saying 'go along the corridor before you go up the stairs' to remind yourself to always give the easting reference first, followed by the northing reference.

Look at Fig. 1.1.2 below. Identify which grid square *Perry Hill* is in.

Step 1: Find *Perry Hill* which is to the north east of *Burpham*.

Step 2: Go to the bottom left hand corner of the grid square that contains Perry Hill.

Step 3: Start by finding the easting reference. Follow the easting (the vertical line) from this point to the end of the line (either at the top or bottom) where you will find its two digit identity number. Write down this number: 05.

Step 4: Now find the northing reference. Return to the bottom left hand corner of the grid square containing *Perry Hill*. Follow the northing (the horizontal line) from this point to the end of the line where you will find its two digit identity number. Write down this number: 09.

Step 5: You should now have a four digit number – 0509 – which is the four figure grid reference for the grid square containing *Perry Hill*. Remember to write down the easting reference first, followed by the northing reference.

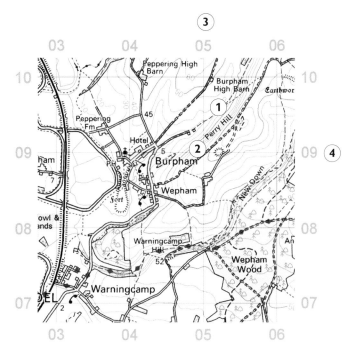

Fig. 1.1.2: Four figure grid references

Here is a reminder of what to do when you are given a grid reference.

Look at Fig. 1.1.3. The grid square you need to find is 0307.

Step 1: Split the grid reference 0307 into two parts: 03 and 07.

Step 2: The first two digit number always refers to the easting. Find easting 03 and put one finger of your right hand on it.

Step 3: The second two digit number always refers to the northing. Find northing 07 and put one finger of your left hand on it.

Step 4: Move both of your fingers along the grid lines until they meet. This is the bottom left hand corner of the grid square you need to find: 0307.

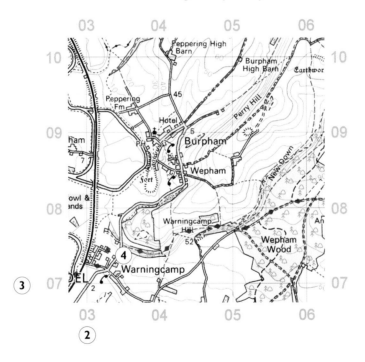

Fig. 1.1.3: Four figure grid references

Using six figure grid references

We use six figure grid references to pinpoint exactly where a given feature is within a grid square. This more accurate grid reference is created by imagining nine extra eastings and nine extra northings within the grid square. This gives you an extra digit to the two digit easting and two digit northing numbers. When they are put together, they create a six figure grid reference. Don't forget to continue to obey the bottom left hand corner rule which you can remember with the saying 'go along the corridor before you go up the stairs'.

Fig. 1.1.4: Six figure grid references

Here is a reminder of what to do when you want to tell someone exactly where something is on a map. Look at Fig. 1.1.4 above. You want to identify precisely where the *public house* is to the north-west of Wepham.

Step 1: Find the *PH (public house)* to the north-west of Wepham.

Step 2: Identify the four figure grid reference for the grid square that the *PH* is in. Your answer should read 0308. If it does not, check again how to do four figure grid references.

Step 3: To find the two extra digits, go to the bottom left hand corner of grid square 0308. For the extra easting digit, imagine nine extra eastings running vertically across the square. These are not normally drawn on maps but are shown in

Fig. 1.1.4 to help you. How many lines across do you have to go before reaching the *PH*? Write this single digit number after the first part of the four figure grid reference (03_). You should have 038.

Step 4: To find the extra northing digit, return to the bottom left hand corner of the grid square containing the *PH*. This time, imagine nine extra northings running horizontally up the square. How many lines up do you have to go before reaching the *PH*? Write this single digit number after the second part of the four figure grid reference (08_). You should have 088.

Step 5: Put the two sets of numbers together, eastings first and then northings. You now have a six figure grid reference for the *PH* to the north-west of Wepham which should read 038088.

Here is a reminder of what to do when you are given a six figure grid reference.

Look at Fig. 1.1.5. Use the following steps to identify the feature at grid reference 051099.

Step 1: Divide the grid reference 051099 into two parts (051 and 099) and underline the first two digits of each set of numbers to find the four figure grid reference first (051 and 099 tell us that the four figure grid reference is 0509).

Step 2: Find the four figure grid reference and put one finger of your right hand and one finger of your left hand on the bottom left hand corner of this grid square.

Step 3: Look again at the first set of numbers: 051. The third digit, the one you have not underlined, tells you how many imaginary extra eastings you need to move across the grid square. Imagine nine extra eastings running across the square and move the finger of your right hand across the grid square to imaginary easting 1. These imaginary eastings are not normally drawn on maps but are in Fig. 1.1.5 to help you. Keep your finger on this point.

Step 4: Look again at the second set of numbers 099. The third digit, the one you have not underlined, tells you how many imaginary extra northings you need to move up the grid square. Imagine nine extra northings running up the square and move the finger of your left hand up the grid square to imaginary northing 9. These imaginary northings are not normally drawn on maps but are shown in Fig. 1.1.5 to help you.

Step 5: Now move your right finger vertically and your left finger horizontally along these imaginary grid lines until they meet. Your fingers should meet at *Burpham High Barn*.

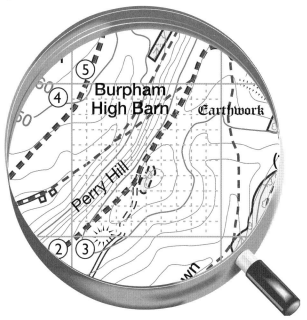

Fig. 1.1.5: Six figure grid references

Identifying direction on OS maps

Remember never to use the words *above*, *below*, *left* or *right* when answering a mapwork question about direction. Instead, use the directions of the eight point compass (Fig. 1.1.6) north, south, east and west. You may want to use the rhyme 'Never Eat Shredded Wheat' to help you remember this.

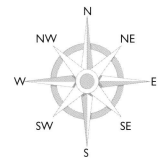

Fig. 1.1.6: The eight point compass

Here is an example. Look at Fig. 1.1.2 (page 5). You would say that the fort at grid reference 038084 is to the *west* of Wepham, *not* to the *left* of Wepham. Remember, when giving the direction of something that lies between the north, south, east and west points, we always say north and south first, *not* east and west (e.g. north-east *not* east-north; south-west *not* west-south). Giving and receiving directions is easy but you must remember to always read the question carefully. Look at the two questions on the next page which refer to Fig. 1.1.2 (on page 5). They look like the same question but the words in italic *to* and *from* mean that the correct answers are in fact opposite to each other.

Question 1: Which direction is it from Burpham *to* Perry Hill?	Question 2: Which direction is Burpham *from* Perry Hill?
Answer 1: North-east	Answer 2: South-west

For precise directions the eight point compass is broken down into the 360 degrees of a circle which we call **bearings**. North has a value of 0 or 360°, east is at 90°, south is at 180° and west is at 270°. To give a bearing as a direction, place your protractor on the map with 0° or 360° facing straight up in a northerly direction, making sure your protractor remains parallel to the eastings. Then, with your protractor fixed in place, use a ruler to line up the features in the question with the centre of your protractor and read the correct bearing off the protractor.

Look at Fig. 1.1.7. Place the centre of your protractor on the *church* in Burpham at grid reference 039090. Remember to place your protractor on the map with the 0° facing straight up in a northerly direction. Find the bearing from the *church* to *Burpham High Barn* at grid reference 051099. You should have a bearing of 50°.

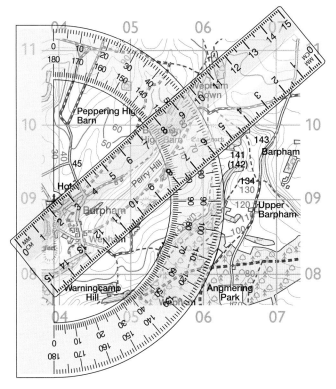

Fig. 1.1.7: Finding a bearing

Measuring distance and area on OS maps

The OS maps you use in exams have scale ratios of either 1:25 000 or 1:50 000, meaning distances on these maps are 25 000 or 50 000 times bigger in real life. You will have already practised your mapwork skills on maps of these scales, but to remind yourself look at the 1:25 000 map of Seaford on page 29 and the 1:50 000 map of Arundel on page 28. Remember that although similar features can be found on both types of maps they have different keys with different symbols. Appendix 1 shows the key from a 1:50 000 scale map (pages 178–179) and the key from a 1:25 000 scale map (pages 176–179). The grid lines on OS maps do not change with the **scale**; a grid square on any OS map at any scale is always 1 km². You can see what scale a map is by looking at the **scale ratio** which can always be found at the bottom of the map.

Below the scale ratio you will find the **scale bar** which helps you convert any distances you measure on the map from centimetres to kilometres (you will need a ruler). Ignore the scale measuring miles; we do not use this. On 1:50 000 scale maps, one centimetre is equal to half a kilometre (500 metres). On 1:25 000 scale maps, one centimetre is equal to a quarter of a kilometre (250 metres). Therefore, when measuring distances in a straight line, or 'as the crow flies', you simply lay your ruler on the map, line up the two points you have been asked to measure the distance between and take a measurement on your ruler. A simple calculation using the scale bar will give you the answer.

For a measured distance taken from a 1:50 000 map divide centimetres by 2 to get kilometres.

For example: measured distance on map 10 cm
actual distance is 10 cm ÷ 2 = 5 km

For a measured distance taken from a 1:25 000 map divide centimetres by 4 to get kilometres.

For example: measured distance on map 12 cm
actual distance is 12 cm ÷ 4 = 3 km

However, you may be asked to measure the distance between two places along a winding route. In this case a ruler will not give you an accurate answer, so you should use a piece of paper or a piece of string to measure the distance along the route, marking points on the edge of the paper, and then place it next to your ruler to get an answer in centimetres. Here is an example:

Look at the 1:50 000 map extract of Arundel on page 28. Measure the distance along the railway track between the stations at the following grid references: 001042 and 026118. You should measure approximately 20 cm which you divide by 2 as this is a 1:50 000 scale map, giving you a measurement of 2 km.

Sometimes you may be asked to work out, or estimate, the size of a particular area on a map.

To do this, you need to remember the following:

on 1:50 000 maps, 1 cm² is equal to 0.25 km² ($\frac{1}{4}$ km²)

on 1:25 000 maps, 1 cm² is equal to 0.0625 km² ($\frac{1}{16}$ km²)

So, to calculate the size of a particular area in km²:

on 1:50 000 maps, divide the number of 1 cm² by 4

on 1:25 000 maps, divide the number of 1 cm² by 16

With this information at hand it is easy to work out the area of square or rectangular shaped areas on the map. However, the **landscape** is rarely so even. Therefore it is more than likely you will have to estimate, with the help of your ruler, how many square centimetres an irregular shaped area covers before making your conversion to kilometres. Here is an example, this time using a map at 1:25 000 scale:

Look at the 1:25 000 map extract of Seaford in Fig 1.1.8 (page 13). Estimate the area covered by buildings in Seaford to the north of the A259 but no further west than easting 48. You do this by imagining each grid square divided into 16 × 1 cm². You then look at each grid square in the area specified and work out as carefully as you can roughly how many 1 cm² are covered in housing. For example, grid square 4900 has about 8 × 1 cm² covered in housing north of the A259; 4899 has about 12 × 1 cm² of housing. Do this for all the grid squares and then calculate how many 1 km² you have in total. You should have around 49 × 1 cm².

We know that 1 cm² on a 1:25 000 map is equivalent to $\frac{1}{16}$ km² so divide 49 by 16 to give an answer of around 3 km².

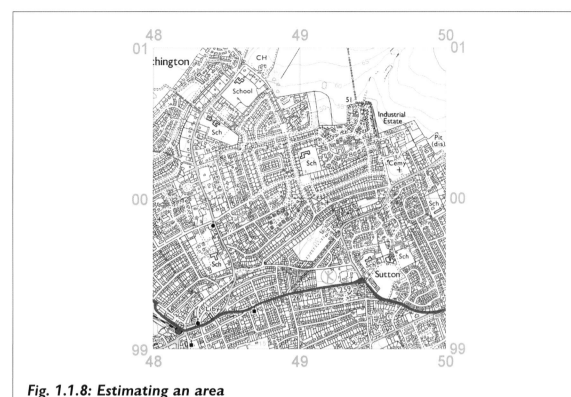

Fig. 1.1.8: Estimating an area

Recognising spot heights, triangulation pillars and contour lines

The height and shape, or relief, of the land is represented in two ways on OS maps. Remember, all heights are given in metres above sea level. Firstly, spot heights are used to give the exact height at a particular point on a map and can be identified by a very small black dot, often but not always on or near a road, with a number written in black ink next to the dot. Look at Fig. 1.1.2 (page 5) at grid reference 042095 and you will see a spot height reading 45 metres above sea level. If a spot height is the highest point in that area of the map it will be surrounded by a blue triangle called a **triangulation pillar**. There may be more than one triangulation pillar on an OS map extract but they will not be located close to each other. Look at the map extract of Arundel on page 28 and you will find, if you look very carefully, four triangulation pillars spread across the map. For example, there is one at 998082.

The second method of representing relief on OS maps is by means of contour lines. These thin brown lines join areas of equal height. On 1:50 000 scale maps a height change of 10 metres divides each contour line whereas on 1:25 000 scale maps a height change of 5 metres divides each contour line. Whether you are using a 1:50 000 or 1:25 000 scale map, remember that when the contour lines are close together a steep **gradient** is being represented and when they are spread further apart it indicates a more gentle relief.

Look at the map of Arundel on page 28. Compare the contour lines in grid square 0505 to the contour lines in grid square 0810 and you should immediately see that the relief is much steeper in grid square 0810 as the contour lines are packed much closer together. Note that the 100 metre contour line in grid square 0810 is thicker than the others around it. This is because on 1:50 000 scale maps the contour lines at every 50 metres are thicker than the others and on 1:25 000 scale maps the contour lines are thicker at 25 metre intervals.

Using contour lines to visualise relief and draw sketch sections

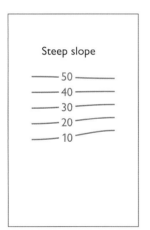

Fig. 1.1.9a: Contour lines depicting a steep slope

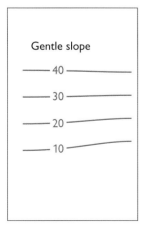

Fig. 1.1.9b: Contour lines depicting a gentle slope

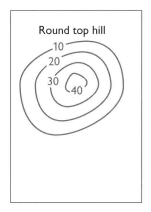

Fig. 1.1.9c: Contour lines for a round top hill

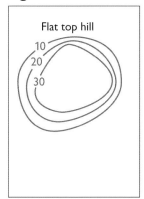

Fig. 1.1.9d: Contour lines for a flat top hill

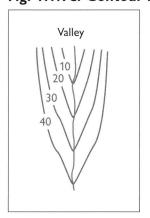

Fig. 1.1.9e: Contour lines for a valley

Fig. 1.1.9: Relief features

Contour lines, and the patterns they create, allow you not only to evaluate the height of the land but also to visualise the shape of the land. It is a very useful skill to be able to recognise contour line patterns which identify **relief features** such as round top hills, flat top hills, valleys and ridges.

Round top hills (Fig. 1.1.9c) are shown by circular contour lines within each other increasing in height steadily towards the peak of the hill or mountain. Flat top hills (Fig. 1.1.9d) are similar to round top hills except the contour lines become much more spread out or disappear towards the centre of the circular shape. This is because after an initial increase in gradient the hill flattens at the top, forming a **plateau** or a **ridge**. Valleys (Fig. 1.1.9e) are illustrated on maps by a 'V' shape pattern of contour lines pointing towards the top of the valley or source of any stream or river flowing in the valley. Can you find examples of any of the relief features shown in Fig. 1.1.9 on the map of Arundel on page 28.

If you can visualise the relief by interpreting the contour lines on a map then you will have no problem in drawing a simple **sketch section** of what you would see from a given point on the map. You are most likely to be asked to draw a sketch section along a northing and between two eastings within a grid square. This means you will need to locate the grid square on the map and then use the contour lines to sketch out the relief of the land as you would see it along the northing. Depending on how many marks there are awarded for the question you might need to add features such as buildings, roads or woodland to your sketch by interpreting map symbols.

Look at the map extract of Seaford on page 29. You are standing on the golf course at grid reference 494983 facing south. Draw a sketch section view of what you would see between easting 49 and easting 50; remember you are facing south! Your sketch should show a ridge rising from 40 to 80 metres with a copse in the eastern section, through which a crossing path runs. You may also include the visible earthworks close to where you are standing in the west (see Fig. 1.1.10).

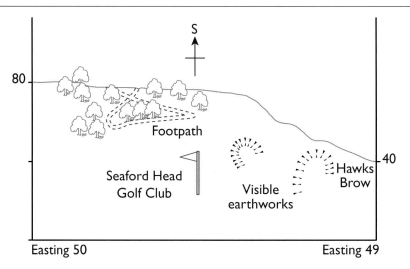

Fig. 1.1.10: Drawing a sketch section

Exam tip

Even if you are under time pressure, try not to rush when working with grid references as it only creates mistakes. If you are given a six figure grid reference you will usually find that the answer is a map feature that cannot be confused with something nearby. Always use the eight points of the compass to indicate direction and be careful to read the question concerning direction carefully; the words *to* and *from* can easily be confused. Remember that spot heights are very small and are sometimes almost hidden by the other information on the map. With contour lines you may need to trace your way round to the point where the height is written or count the number of lines up or down to find the value of the contour line you are looking at.

Summary

- Whether completing four figure or six figure grid references, remember to choose the bottom number first (the easting) and then the number from the side (the northing), 'go along the corridor before you go up the stairs'. Where these lines meet on the map is the bottom left hand corner of the grid square.

- Below the scale ratio on OS maps there will be a scale bar that allows you to work out how far 1 centimetre on the map is in real life in kilometres. Use the scale bar to work out distances on a map using a ruler if the question asks for a distance 'as the crow flies', or using a piece of paper or a piece of string if you are asked to follow a winding route. Be careful when measuring off distances against the scale bar as 0 km is often in the middle.

- Spot heights are the exact height at a specific point on the map.

- A triangulation pillar is a spot height surrounded by a blue triangle, meaning that this point is the highest point in the area.

- Contour lines link areas of equal height. Together, contour lines can also show the relief of the land by the patterns they make.

Exercise 1A

All questions refer either to the map extract of Arundel on page 28 or to the map extract of Seaford on page 29. You may need to refer to the keys (pages 176–179) to find the answers to these questions.

1. Name a feature you can find on the map of Arundel in the following grid squares:
   (a) 0704   (c) 0610
   (b) 0109   (d) 0004

2. (a) There are eleven schools on the map of Seaford. Give the six figure grid reference for five of them.
   (b) For the five you have chosen, list which direction each school lies from the leisure centre at grid reference 493994.

3. What job would you do if you worked in Seaford at the following grid references:
   (a) 481991   (c) 506995
   (b) 494982   (d) 485985

4. (a) How far is it 'as the crow flies' from Whiteways Lodge on the Arundel map at grid reference 003107 to the Public House (PH) just to the west of Hammerpot at grid reference 066057?
   (b) How far would it be if you measured this distance along the road taking the A284 followed by the A27?

5. Describe the relief of Arundel Park which can be found to the north-west of Arundel.

Exercise 1B

All questions refer either to the map extract of Arundel on page 28 or to the map extract of Seaford on page 29. You may need to refer to the keys (pages 176–179) to find the answers to these questions.

1. Give the six figure grid references and heights of all four triangulation pillars that appear on the Arundel map extract.

2. Identify the relief features at the following grid references on the Arundel map extract:
   (a) 017087   (c) 081101
   (b) 070090   (d) 995077

3. Estimate the area covered by sea on the map extract of Seaford (page 29).

4. Using the map of Arundel (page 28), compare the relief in the north-east of this map extract to the relief in the south-west of the extract.

5. You are standing facing east at grid reference 470006 on the Seaford map. Draw a sketch section of what you would see between northing 003 and northing 008.

1.2 Map symbols showing human and physical features

Common map symbols – syllabus extra/scholarship

Geography exams require you to answer a lot of questions in a short period, so it is useful to find ways of saving time.

To save time in the mapwork section of an exam it is useful to learn the common map symbols that you may well be asked to identify. Learning some of these symbols will save you valuable minutes as you won't have to turn the map over to identify the symbol on the key.

There are particular map symbols for 1:25 000 maps and 1:50 000 maps – see Appendix I on pages 176–179. Try to familiarise yourself with as many of the symbols as you can from these keys. Here is a useful selection of symbols from each.

Symbol	Meaning	Key category
	Viewpoint	Tourist and leisure
	Information centre (all year/seasonal)	Tourist and leisure
	Country park	Tourist and leisure
	Nature reserve	Tourist and leisure
	Off road cycle routes	Other public access
	National Trail/Recreational route	Other public access
	Places of worship (churches)	General features
	Youth hostel	General features
	Orchard	Vegetation
	Marsh, reeds or saltings	Vegetation

Fig. 1.2.1: Selected map symbols from 1:25 000 maps

Symbol	Meaning	Key category
 P P&R P&R	Parking, Park and ride, all year/seasonal	Tourist information
	Golf course or links	Tourist information
	Telephone, public/motoring organisation	Tourist information
 X	Camp site/Caravan site	Tourist information
P	Post office	Abbreviations
PH	Public house	Abbreviations
	National Park	Boundaries
	National Trust – always open	Land features
....	Footpath	Public rights of way
--------	Bridleway	Public rights of way

Fig 1.2.2: Selected map symbols from 1:50 000 maps

Identifying human and physical features

Features on maps are split into two different groups. **Physical features** are those things on the map that are clearly natural, such as an area of wild woodland, a river, the sea or hills and valleys. Any feature on the map that is in some way man-made is called a **human feature**, for example roads, schools, railway lines and stations. Whether identifying human or physical features, always try to refer to something specific rather than giving a general answer. Look at Fig. 1.2.3 (page 21). In grid square 0978 we can identify several specific physical features such as valleys, streams and a steep hillside. Check you can identify each one of these correctly. Use the 1:50 000 scale in Appendix 1 to remind you. In grid square 0876 we can identify several human features such as the paper mill, a pier, the railway line and the A830 main road.

It is important to make sure you do not give ambiguous answers when asked to identify physical or human features on a map. Do not choose a feature that could be physical or human. Here is an example. Look at Fig. 1.2.3 (page 21). The coniferous woodland in the north west section of the map could be interpreted as a physical or human feature as this type of woodland is usually a man-made plantation. Other features that could be ambiguous include man-made lakes or reservoirs and canals.

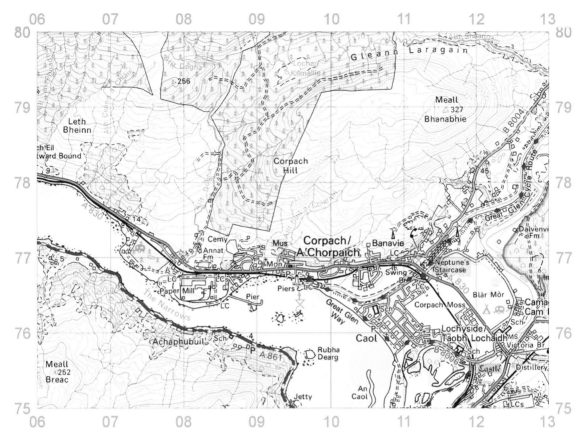

Fig. 1.2.3: OS map extract of Fort William

Describing routes

A good knowledge of map symbols and their meanings is useful when a question asks you to describe a route across an OS map. The examiner will be looking for accuracy in your description and will allocate marks for identification of physical and human features along the journey. You should also make reference to the altitude. The route may be a short walk of a few kilometres along a footpath on the map or may be a longer journey following a road or railway and you should identify the distance travelled.

Look at the map extract from the Peak District on page 31. Imagine you were asked to describe what you would see from a boat travelling down the River Noe from where the river enters the map in grid square 1783 to where it leaves the map in grid square 1882. Physical features you would see include the flat valley floor (floodplain), woodland and river meanders. Human features you would pass include bridges, a sewage works, a mill and a caravan/campsite. Do not forget to use the directions of the eight point compass rather than the using the words up, down, left and right, and give precise grid references where possible (e.g. the mill on the north bank of the river at grid reference 173837).

> **Exam tip**
> Remember to go for obviously man-made structures when asked to identify a human feature on the map, such as a specific building like a school, church or post office. If it is a physical feature you are looking for, remember the different relief features that contour lines represent. Whether it is a human or physical feature you are asked for, make sure you don't give an ambiguous answer.

Summary

It is the symbols on the map that give you all the detail about what a place is like and it is worth learning many of the most commonly used map symbols (Appendix 1 on pages 176–179). All features represented on OS maps can be split into:

- physical features – natural parts of the landscape
- human features – man-made aspects of the landscape.

 Exercise 1C

Questions 1 and 2 refer to the 1:50 000 map extract of the Isle of Wight on page 30. Questions 3 and 4 refer to the 1:25 000 map extract of the Peak District on page 31.

1. Look at the Isle of Wight map on page 30. What is the meaning of the map symbols at the following grid references?
   (a) 547777   (b) 548797   (c) 533782

2. Give the four figure grid reference of any caravan/campsite on the map.

3. Look at the map of the Peak District on page 31. Give three pieces of map evidence that suggest tourism is important in this area.

4. Follow the A6187 from the car park in Castleton (149832) to the campsite north-east of Brough (186828). Describe two physical and two human features you would see out of the window if you were making this journey in a car.

 Exercise 1D

1. Using the Isle of Wight map extract on page 30, identify with a six figure grid reference one example of each of the 1:50 000 symbols listed in Fig. 1.2.2. (page 20), with the exception of a National Park.

2. Look at the map extract from the Peak District on page 31. Describe the fastest route on foot between Bradwell 1781 and Castleton 1582. Refer to physical and human features you would pass on your journey.

1.3 How OS maps can be used to study other topics

Geography exams often demand that you use your map skills throughout the paper. After you have completed the Mapwork section of the exam, don't be tempted to fold up the OS map and think you can get on with the rest of the paper without using it. The map can be used in relation to questions in other sections of the paper, so leave it out on your desk.

Weathering, erosion, rivers and coasts

Most OS maps have either a river or a section of coastline on them so it is likely that a question regarding rivers or coasts will refer to the map. The questions could ask you about the formation of lowland or upland river features such as V-shaped valleys, waterfalls, meanders and ox-bow lakes or how coastal features such as headlands, bays and spits are created. The question could examine your knowledge of three types of weathering (physical or mechanical weathering, freeze-thaw and onion skin, biological and chemical weathering; these are discussed further in Chapter 2) by asking you which process is likely to occur at a given point on the map and why. Your understanding of drainage may be tested by a question asking you to describe or analyse the drainage on the map provided.

Weather and climate

Within the topic of *weather and climate,* only the subject of microclimate is likely to be related to the OS map you are provided with. You may be asked to discuss the influences in a specific location on the OS map of human and physical features such as buildings, woodland, lakes, etc. on temperature and rainfall readings. You may need to consider how relief, indicated by the contour lines on the map, may also affect local temperature and precipitation readings due to the height of the land and also its aspect.

Economic activities

As a 'human geography' topic, economic activities can also be easily related to the OS map you have with your exam paper. You are most likely to be asked to identify a primary, secondary or tertiary industry from the map.

- Farms or woodland plantations that might be used for forestry are examples of **primary industry**.

- Industrial estates or 'works' indicate **secondary industry**.

- Schools, hospitals, hotels, shopping centres, tourist information centres and museums are all examples of **tertiary industry**.

Environmental issues

Quite often you will find that the OS map extract you have with your exam paper covers an area that is popular with tourists. The reason for this is that tourists are usually attracted to areas of natural beauty and such areas contain a variety of geographical features that you could be tested on in an exam. This is why it is particularly important to have a good knowledge of tourist-related map symbols.

Tourism puts pressure on the environment and may conflict with the environment. For example, tourists walking off pathways in National Parks may cause soil erosion, damaging the very environment they have come to enjoy. Settlement growth, urban sprawl, and the demand for new houses is another example of how the environment may be damaged as a result of a pressure placed upon it.

Therefore, if you are asked to refer to the map in an 'environmental issues' question you are likely to be asked to discuss or give evidence of environmental pressures the area may receive.

Settlement

Your knowledge of the site, situation and shape of settlements will be tested in the mapwork section of the CE paper. The next chapter explains how in more detail.

Exam tip

After you have completed the questions in the mapwork section of the exam, leave your OS map open on your desk. At some point, and often more than once, you will have to refer back to the OS map in order to answer other questions (e.g. weather and climate). When asked to find map evidence, always give a four or six figure grid reference and justify your choice of evidence.

Summary

Of all the skills you need to do well in Geography exams, being able to interpret and use an OS map is probably the most important. This is because the OS map not only has a section of questions itself in the paper but can also be referred to in any part of the paper. So, even if you are an expert at a topic such as weather and climate, if your mapwork skills are not up to scratch you may not achieve as high marks as you expect in that section. For example, imagine trying to answer the questions in Exercises 1E and 1F if you were unable to locate the areas on the map referred to in the questions.

Level
1

Exercise 1E

Look at Fig. 1.3.1 (below), taken from a map extract of Exeter.

1. Look at the River Clyst in grid squares 9689 and 9789. What will happen to this section of the river in the future?

2. What is the name of the flat land that is either side of the River Clyst? Why are there no buildings on this land, and what do you think it will be used for? Give reasons for your answer.

3. What do you think would be the difference in night-time temperatures taken in grid squares 9392 and 9789? Explain your answer.

4. The school in grid square 9490 is built on the south-facing slope of Pyne's Hill. What effect is this going to have on temperature readings at the school and what else could influence how warm or cold it is at a school?

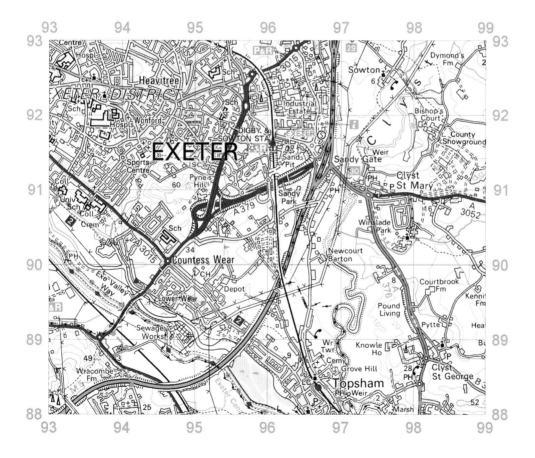

Fig. 1.3.1: OS map extract of Exeter

5.   A supermarket covering 100 m² is to be built in or near Exeter. Give the six figure grid reference of the site you would choose and three reasons for your choice.

6.   Describe the drainage to the east of easting 97.

Exercise 1F

Look at the map extract of the Isle of Wight on page 30 for questions 1–3, 5 and 6, and the map extract of the Peak District on page 31 for question 4.

1.   In grid square 5882 groynes enter the sea. Describe the process groynes are designed to stop.

2.   Describe the types of coastal erosion that might have created Luccombe Bay and Horse Ledge in grid squares 5879 and 5880.

3.   What type of weathering do you think would occur on Shanklin Down 567801? Describe the stages of this process (you may find it useful to refer to Chaper 2 of this book).

4.   If you were going to build a weather station within 1 km of Castleton, where would you put it and why?

5.   Find and give the four figure grid reference of an example of a primary industry and a tertiary industry on the map extract of the Isle of Wight.

6.   (You may find it useful to refer to Chapter 4 for this question.)
     (a) What settlement pattern are Shanklin and Ventnor on the Isle of Wight map?
     (b) Why are they this settlement pattern?
     (c) List examples, with their four figure grid references, of settlements on the Isle of Wight map that have different settlement patterns from Shanklin and Ventnor.

7.   What evidence is there that different industries are placing pressure on the environment? Make reference to examples in both maps.

Exercise 1G: Enquiry suggestion

Use all the map skills you have acquired in this section to make a map of your school grounds or even part of your local town or village. Your teacher will direct you to the focus of your task. To help you with analysing what human and physical features are in the given area, you may want to refer to satellite imagery of your chosen area and satellite generated maps which can be found on websites such as www.bing.com/maps and www.google.com/earth. To work out the height of the land in order to add spot heights or contour lines to your map your teacher may provide you with suitable measuring equipment such as ranging poles and clinometers.

Exercise 1H: Past exam questions

Look at the OS map of the Peak District on page 31. All the questions below are taken from the February 2004 Common Entrance paper.

1. What do you find at 149828 and 153810? (2 marks)

2. In which direction does the River Noe flow? What map evidence shows this? (3 marks)

3. What is the distance by road from the junction at Goosehill (144828) to the church at Hope (172835)? Remember to answer in kilometres. (2 marks)

4. Give evidence to show how there have been changes in land use west of easting 16. (2 marks)

The following four pages contain the map extracts for Arundel, Seaford, Isle of Wight and the Peak District.

Exercise 1I

Solve the following clues.

1. A geographer who makes maps (12 letters)
2. … pillar. Spot height surrounded by a blue triangle indicating the highest point in that area on the map (13 letters)
3. A list of all the symbols used on a map and their meanings (3 letters)
4. Elevated area of high land (7 letters)
5. Direction split up into 360° (8 letters)
6. The shape and height of the land (6 letters)
7. Term used to describe the steepness of a slope (8 letters)
8. A black dot on an OS map with a number giving its height above sea level in metres (4 letters + 6 letters)
9. A blue grid line running up and down an OS map (7 letters)

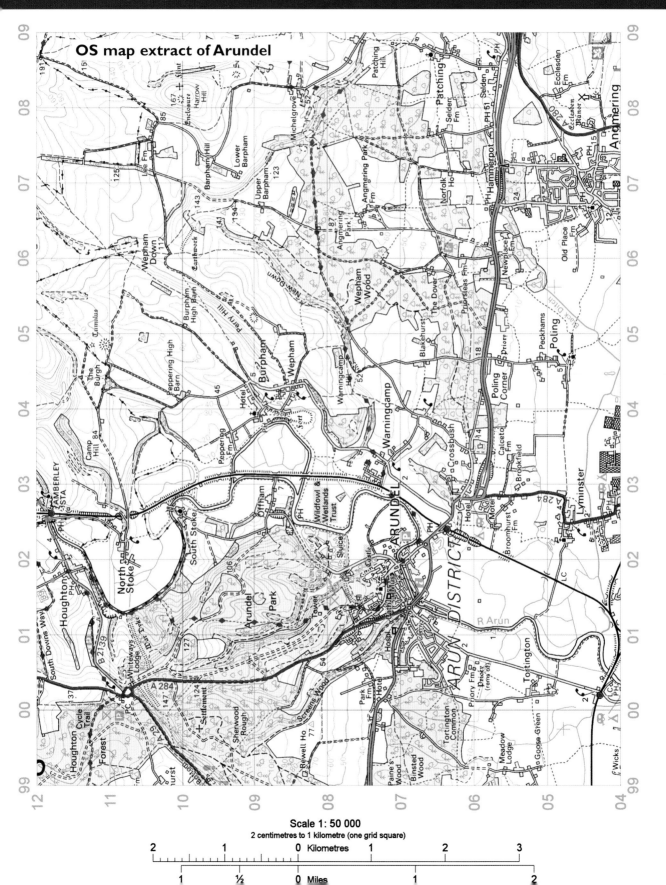

OS map extract of Arundel

Scale 1: 50 000
2 centimetres to 1 kilometre (one grid square)

2   1   0 Kilometres   1   2   3

1   ½   0 Miles   1   2

OS map extract of Seaford

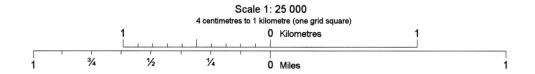

Scale 1: 25 000

4 centimetres to 1 kilometre (one grid square)

OS map extract of the Isle of Wight

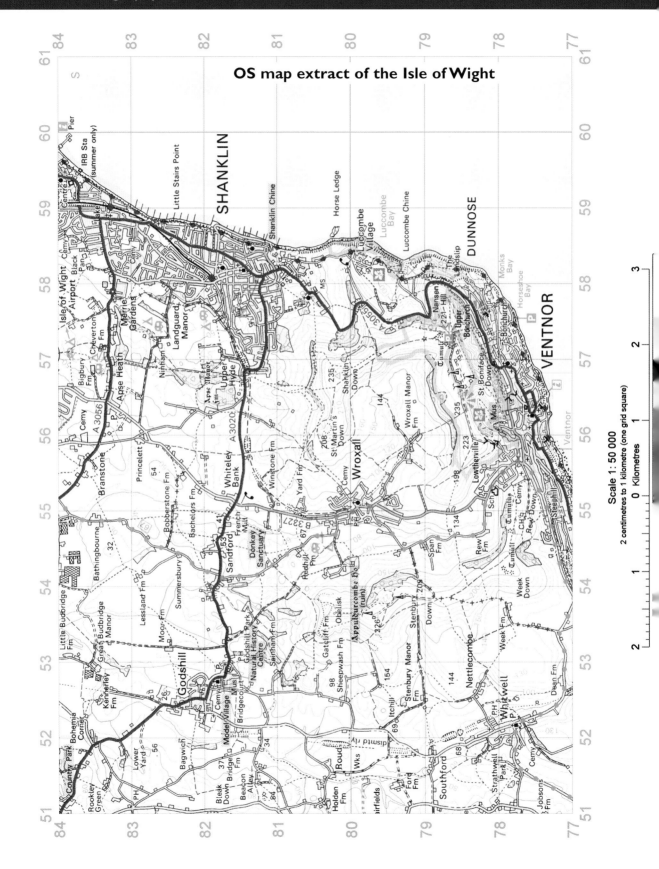

Scale 1 : 50 000

2 centimetres to 1 kilometre (one grid square)

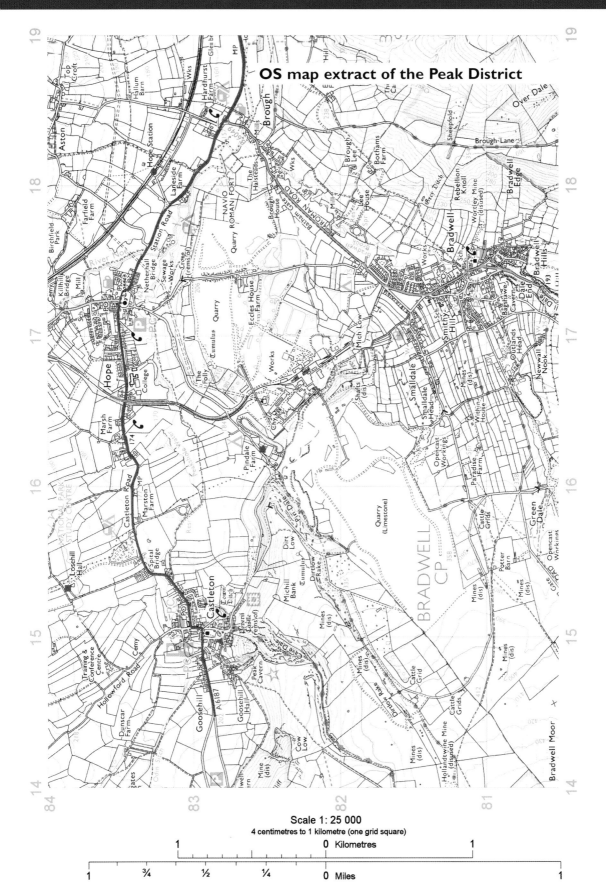

OS map extract of the Peak District

Scale 1 : 25 000
4 centimetres to 1 kilometre (one grid square)

1   0   Kilometres   1

1   ¾   ½   ¼   0   Miles   1

Mapwork glossary

Bearing	Compass direction given in degrees (360° in the complete circle).
Contour line	A brown line on a map joining places of the same height together.
Easting	A vertical blue grid line on an OS map.
Four figure grid reference	A set of two two-digit numbers indicating the grid square in which an object is located on an OS map.
Gradient	Term used to describe the steepness of a slope.
Grid squares	The area of 1 kilometre square created by the grid lines on an OS map.
Human features	Man-made features such as schools and churches.
Key	A list of all the symbols used on a map and their meanings.
Landscape	The natural and human features of an area.
Northing	A horizontal blue grid line on an OS map.
Physical features	Natural features such as rivers and hills.
Plateau	An elevated area of high land with a relatively flat surface.
Primary industry	Taking raw materials from the land and the sea. These tend to be very large and old industries such as farming, fishing, mining and forestry.
Relief	The shape and height of the land.
Relief features	Different landforms illustrated by the shape of the contour lines.
Ridge	A long area of elevated land with a crest.
Scale	The ratio difference between real size and actual size on a map.
Scale bar	A ruler which shows real distances on the map, usually found at the bottom of an OS map.
Scale ratio	A ratio which shows how much bigger features on the map are in real life.
Secondary industry	Industries that manufacture or process the raw materials collected in the primary industries, such as food processing, car assembly and oil refining.

Six figure grid reference	A set of two three-digit numbers indicating the exact location of an object on an OS map.
Sketch section	An outline of the relief of a landscape based on an approximation of what the contour lines are showing, and annotated to show the main features.
Spot height	A black dot on an OS map with a number giving its height above sea level in metres.
Tertiary industry	Industries that are involved in selling (retailing), such as supermarkets and department stores, as well as all industries providing services, such as entertainment, finance, health and education.
Triangulation pillar	Spot height surrounded by a blue triangle indicating the highest point in that area on the map.

Chapter 2: Landform processes

A spectacular waterfall, the result of rock formations   *A river delta*

Flooding in Boscastle, Cornwall (2004)   *Stack and arch formation*

In this chapter we will cover:

- The processes of weathering and erosion, and how rock type affects the speed of these processes acting on the land.

- How the different processes of weathering combine with the river processes of erosion, transportation and deposition to create river features such as waterfalls, meanders and deltas.

- How the different processes of weathering combine with coastal processes of erosion, transportation and deposition to create coastal features such as headlands and spits.

- The triggers of major flooding in the world and the causes and human responses to the Pakistan floods in 2010.

2.1 Weathering and erosion

What is the difference between weathering and erosion?

This is a good question, and one you may well be asked in an exam! If you look around your house or school you may notice that some of the brickwork, stone or tarmac appears to be cracking and breaking up (Fig. 2.1.1 below). This is the effect of weather on the surface of the buildings and is called **weathering**. Weathering also occurs on natural surfaces such as mountains or cliffs. **Erosion** is a different process which takes place when a force, such as a fast flowing river, rubs against rock such as the stone surface that makes the river's bed and banks. The wind, human and animal movements, the sea and glaciers are all other forces that can cause erosion. Weathering and erosion often combine to create features on our landscape such as valleys.

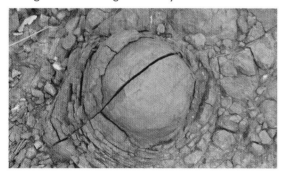

Biological weathering caused by tree roots

Physical or mechanical weathering: Onion-skin weathering in a desert

Chemical weathering on a gargoyle

Fig. 2.1.1: Evidence of weathering around us

Remember the differences between weathering and erosion:

- Weathering is the breakdown of rock by the weather, plants and animals.

- Erosion is the breakdown and removal of rock by rivers, sea and ice.

Types of weathering

There are four distinct types of weathering that you need to know about. They may act separately or together over time to break down a rock surface, and may also combine with processes of erosion to help create landform features. Fig. 2.1.2 below explains each type of weathering.

Physical or mechanical: Freeze-thaw	Physical or mechanical: Onion skin	Chemical	Biological
1. Rocks have cracks in them. 	1. Sun heats rocks in deserts to 40°C...  ...causing it to expand.	1. Rain water contains a weak acid. 	1. Tree roots can grow into the cracks of rocks. 
2. Relief rainfall in mountains gets into cracks. 	2. Rock in desert cools at night to 0°C, causing it to contract. 	2. When rain lands on softer rocks like limestone the acid reacts with a chemical in the rock causing some of it to dissolve. *Today* 	Tree roots expand gradually, increasing the pressure in the rocks and causing the cracks to widen.
3. At night water freezes and expands by 10%, widening crack. 	3. Continual expansion and contraction over thousands of years creates layers in the rock. 	*200 years' time* 	2. Seeds can fall into cracks and germinate. 
4. In the day the ice melts. 	4. Layers peel off like the skin of an onion. 	3. Chemical weathering can commonly be seen on grave stones and gargoyles.	3. Animals can burrow into soil, causing areas to collapse. 
5. This happens again and again and breaks up the rock. 			
6. Scree slopes are left.			

Fig. 2.1.2: The four types of weathering

1. Physical or mechanical: Freeze-thaw weathering

This processes of weathering is easy to understand. It is visible if you go out walking in the mountains and is an excellent form of weathering to explain in an exam using well-labelled diagrams. It is sometimes referred to as **frost-shattering**.

Freeze-thaw weathering occurs in mountainous areas that receive a lot of rainfall (relief rainfall) and experience a **temperature range** either side of 0°C. Water will flow into the cracks, which occur in all types of rocks, after rainfall. During the night, temperatures may fall below freezing, causing the water in the cracks to freeze. When water freezes it expands by approximately 10% which therefore widens the crack and puts pressure on the rock surface. In the morning, the temperature may rise above zero, allowing the ice to melt and the water to trickle away. This process may be repeated again and again, night after night, over hundreds and thousands of years. Eventually the cracks in the rock will be so wide that it will collapse. The collapsed rock may tumble down a slope and settle at the base of the mountain with other weathered material. This can be called **mass movement** and the collection of loose weathered material is called a **scree** and typically forms into a slope.

2. Physical or mechanical: Onion-skin weathering

This process, also known as **exfoliation**, usually occurs in hot and dry areas and so is particularly obvious in desert environments. In deserts the temperature can rise up to 40°C during the day and can fall back down to 0°C at night. This large temperature range means that the surface of any rock outcrop experiences a large amount of expansion then contraction due to the heating of the sun over a 24-hour period. The outer layers of a rock surface will heat up and cool down (expand and contract) most as they are nearer to the Sun's rays. Over many years this continual expansion and contraction will cause the outer layer of rock to become detached from the rock surface and peel off, a bit like the outer layer of an onion, hence the name **onion-skin weathering** (Fig. 2.1.1 page 35).

3. Chemical weathering

The speed at which all processes of weathering occur depends on the rock type the weathering is acting upon. This is of particular importance in chemical weathering because this process requires the rock to have a mineral within it that reacts with rainwater. Rainwater has a weak acid in it. As it falls on a rock surface the weak acid in the rainwater may react with a mineral in the rock and slowly dissolve the rock surface. Limestone contains a mineral called calcium carbonate which can be dissolved by the weak acid in rainwater. Evidence of this can be seen on gravestones, which are often made from limestone, with older gravestones losing the detail of their inscriptions due to their surfaces dissolving. Similarly, ornate gargoyles decorating old buildings in cities such as Cambridge and Oxford have lost their detail due to **chemical weathering** (Fig. 2.1.1 page 35).

4. Biological weathering

If you have ever tried to pull a plant or tree root out of the ground you will have realised how strong roots can be. Plants and trees are very adaptable and can grow almost anywhere where there is moisture and sunlight. Roots can grow into the cracks of rocks and, like ice expanding the cracks of rocks in the process of freeze-thaw weathering, the roots widen the cracks over many years and can make the rock crumble. If you look carefully you might be able to see evidence of the pavement in your street or tarmac around your school beginning to break up due to the action of tree roots. Animals burrowing beneath rocks and causing rock to overhang and possibly collapse is another form of **biological weathering**.

Erosion and transportation in the river basin

As a river flows from highland to lowland, it will act as a force upon its bed and banks, eroding the rock that forms the **channel**. Erosion is most evident in highland because the river has a higher level of energy as it rushes down steep slopes. This steep **gradient** causes the water to froth up. This is given the name white water, as in 'white water rafting'. However, erosion can take place at any point within the river – even in lowland, especially when the river is in flood. When a river erodes its bed and banks it will move the eroded material downstream, a process known as **transportation**. We call the eroded material transported downstream by a river its **load**.

There are four different types of erosion that act on and widen the channel and five types of transportation. Try to avoid mixing them up.

The four types of erosion

1. Hydraulic action

This is the action of river water hitting the bed and banks, wearing them away and widening the channel. This is most likely to be significant in highland when the water is flowing quickly down a steep gradient.

2. Abrasion

Any load carried by the river will be forced by the flow of water to hit the bed and banks, further wearing it away and widening the channel. Again, abrasion will be more significant in highland when the river is flowing fast down a steep gradient.

3. Attrition

Any load carried by the river will hit the bed and banks (abrasion) and collide with itself, causing it to break into smaller particles. This will result in pebbles being carried by the river becoming smoother and rounder as they are transported downstream.

4. Corrosion (solution)

This is the process by which smaller particles are dissolved into the river. It may occur in any part of the river's course, depending upon the type of rock over which the river is flowing. A river is filled by rainwater which has a mild acid within it. As the water flows over the rock surface it may dissolve minerals contained within the rock. For example, limestone contains the mineral calcium carbonate which is dissolved by the mild acid in rainwater, and subsequently river water, as in chemical weathering.

The five types of transportation

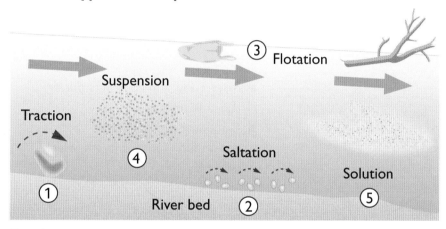

Fig. 2.1.3: The five types of transportation

1. Traction

Large boulders and rocks are rolled along the bed of the river when it has a large amount of energy. This often occurs in highland when the river has a high level of energy due to the steep gradient it is flowing down, or may occur in the lower course of a river when it is in flood.

2. Saltation

Smaller pebbles are bounced along the channel, rolling downstream or leapfrogging over one another with the flow of the water. Abrasion and attrition will occur as the load is transported downstream by saltation.

3. Flotation

Any load that is able to float will be carried downstream by flotation; typically this will be branches of trees and often litter.

4. Suspension

The river not only erodes the rock surface of the channel but also the soil on the banks. Soil particles are then held within the water, often making it look a murky brown colour. This process of transportation is commonly seen in the lower course of a river.

5. Solution

Following corrosion, dissolved minerals will be transported downstream within the water. This is known as solution and can occur in any part of the river's course depending on the rock type over which it is flowing.

Revision tip

You could revise the subject of weathering or indeed any topic by drawing a spider/star diagram. The example below summarises the types of weathering. Make sure all the facts you need to know are included.

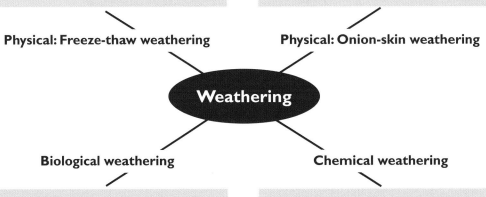

Physical: Freeze-thaw weathering
- Water flows into cracks in rock.
- Water freezes and expands at night.
- Ice melts during the day.
- Continual expansion and contraction widens gaps.
- Eventually rocks fall apart.

Physical: Onion-skin weathering
- Rock expands in heat of desert during the day.
- Rock cools and contracts during the cold night.
- Continual expansion and contraction loosens layers, which peel off.

Weathering

Biological weathering
- Tree roots grow into the cracks of rocks.
- Roots grow and widen the cracks.
- Seeds fall into cracks and germinate.
- Animals can burrow underneath rocks, causing a collapse.

Chemical weathering
- Rainwater containing light acid reacts with minerals in stonework.
- Surface of stone slowly dissolves away.
- Hard edges are smoothed off and carved features become indistinct.

Exam tip

If you are given the choice of a type of weathering to explain in the exam, it is a good idea to choose freeze-thaw weathering. It is easy to draw diagrams to explain what happens and there are several parts to the process which are simple to understand and explain. Often the map included with the exam paper will be of a mountainous region so you can make reference to an example area of where freeze-thaw weathering may occur and say why you think this would be the case.

Summary

Weathering and erosion are two separate processes that act together to shape our landscape. Different types of weathering are likely to occur in different types of environment; for example, onion-skin weathering will be more significant in hotter areas such as deserts. The rate at which weathering and erosion occur is influenced by the rock type: softer, less resistant rocks will be weathered and eroded at a faster rate.

Exercise 2A

1. What is the difference between weathering and erosion?

2. Write a sentence to explain the meaning of the following words:

   transportation   load   channel

3. Create a flow chart with at least four parts to describe what happens in each process of weathering.

4. Draw a labelled diagram showing two processes of erosion. Give your diagram a title and underneath it say where these two types of erosion are likely to occur in the course of a river.

Exercise 2B

1. Write a paragraph to describe what evidence there is at your school or at your home to suggest different types of weathering are at work.

2. Describe how and why a river's load changes shape by the time it reaches its lower course. Refer to processes of erosion and transportation in your answer.

Extension question

3. The following processes of erosion and transportation are often found in the same part of the river. Explain why.
   - **abrasion** and **saltation**
   - **corrosion** and **solution**
   - **hydraulic action** and **traction**

4.   What factors do you believe could vary the speed of weathering in given locations around the world?

2.2 River system features

The area of land that is drained by a river is called its drainage or **river basin** (Fig. 2.2.1 below). A river basin is usually separated from other river basins by a ridge of highland called a **watershed**. The river begins in highland at its **source**, which could be a spring, a glacier or a lake. As the river flows towards the sea it is joined by other rivers called **tributaries**; the point where a tributary joins the main river is called a **confluence**. As the river nears the sea it widens as the river flow meets the tide from the sea. This wide area of fresh and salt (brackish) water is called the **estuary**. The river finally flows out of its **mouth** into the sea where it drops much of the load it has been carrying, sometimes forming a **delta**.

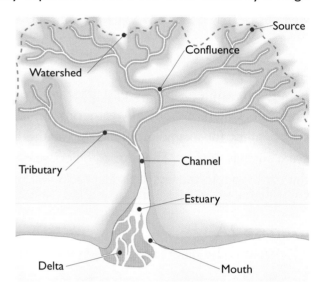

Fig. 2.2.1: Features of a river basin

Three processes occur throughout the course of a river as it flows from highland to lowland: erosion, transportation and **deposition**. Deposition is the name given to the process of a river dropping the load it is transporting as it slows down.

Highland river features

The river has a high level of energy in highland as it is flowing fast over a steep gradient. **Vertical erosion** will occur here as the river erodes the river channel by hydraulic action and abrasion, creating features such as waterfalls and V-shaped valleys. Further downstream in lowland the river will start to move from side to side, causing **lateral erosion** and the formation of meanders and ox-bow lakes. As the river flows over lowland, it will deposit its load at places where the flow of water is slow and therefore the river has little energy. Such places include the inside bend of **meanders** and the mouth where deltas are formed.

Upland river features

V-shaped valleys

Fig. 2.2.2: V-shaped valley – Sail Beck, north-western fells of the Lake District

If you have been to a mountainous region of Britain such as North Wales or the Lake District (Fig. 2.2.2 above) you will have noticed that between the mountains are steep-sided **V-shaped valleys**. V-shaped valleys are a result of river erosion and weathering. We can split the formation of a V-shaped valley into four stages (Fig. 2.2.3 on page 44) which combine the processes of erosion, weathering and transportation. It takes thousands of years for a V-shaped valley to form. It is a slow process that is even slower if it is taking place within hard, resistant rock. All four steps occur simultaneously but it is easier to understand how the V-shaped valley forms if we put them into an order.

Stage 1

The river in highland areas has very little energy to erode sideways but does erode vertically by hydraulic action and abrasion, by flowing over steep slopes into its bed. This vertical erosion creates a steep narrow gorge.

Stage 2

The exposed sides of the steep narrow gorge are moistened by spray from the fast-flowing river and, because they are located in the mountains, they also receive relief rainfall. A temperature range either side of zero and this moisture means that the exposed sides are liable to being attacked and broken down by freeze-thaw and, depending on the rock type, chemical weathering.

Stage 3

A combination of gravity and rainwater wash the weathered material into the river. New slopes are created to form the V-shaped valley. New slopes on the V-shaped valley are called **spurs.** Spurs are a feature of highland streams and rivers near the source.

Stage 4

The weathered material which is washed into the river becomes the river's load and is transported downstream by the processes of traction and saltation.

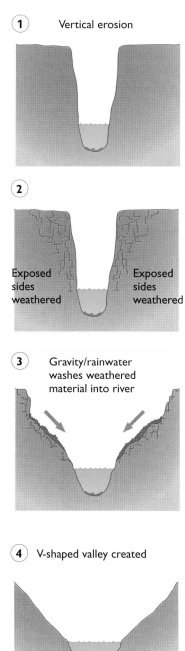

Fig. 2.2.3: Stages of formation of a V-shaped valley

River's load transported downstream

Waterfalls

If you follow a river towards its source up a V-shaped valley you may find a **waterfall.** A waterfall is caused when there is a difference in the height of land over which a river flows. This difference may have been caused by the movement of the earth's plates, or because a glacier had deepened a valley leaving tributaries hanging above their confluences. One of the most common causes of waterfalls is a river flowing over rock types of different resistance. As with the V-shaped valley, it is easier to understand the formation of waterfalls if we look at the process in stages (Fig. 2.2.4 below).

Stages 1, 2 and 3

The land upon which we walk and rivers flow is a complex mixture of different rock types; some rocks are soft such as clay or sandstone and some are hard such as granite. If a river in highland, which has a lot of power to erode vertically, flows over an area where soft and hard rock meet, the softer less resistant rock will erode more quickly. Due to the different speeds of erosion a small step and then a larger step will form. Eventually the step will be significant enough for the water to begin falling down onto the lower level of the soft rock. This may be known as a **rapid** and will cause a frothing up of the water to make white water.

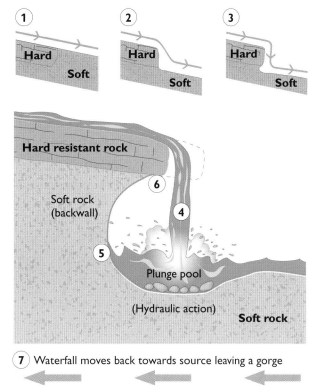

Fig. 2.2.4: Stages of formation of a waterfall

Stage 4

The river water falling onto the lower level of soft rock will scrape out a bowl called a **plunge pool** through hydraulic action, corrosion and possibly abrasion if there is sufficient load in the plunge pool.

Stage 5

The further the river water falls, the more spray will be created when it hits the plunge pool. This spray will hit the softer rock of the back wall of the waterfall and lead to its erosion by corrosion, abrasion and hydraulic action.

Stage 6

As the back wall recedes, a larger and larger section of harder, resistant rock will overhang the waterfall. Gravity will eventually mean that the overhanging rock collapses and falls into the plunge pool.

Stage 7
After the overhang has collapsed, the river water will then fall slightly nearer to the source and cause the whole waterfall to retreat upstream, leaving behind it a very steep-sided valley called a **gorge**.

Lowland river features

As a river flows from highland to lowland it starts to flow over more gentle gradients. This means the river gradually stops eroding downwards (vertical erosion) and begins to erode from side to side (lateral erosion). The river moves from side to side more and more as it nears the sea, creating a large area of flat land either side of the river called the **floodplain** (see Fig. 2.2.6 page 47). As many tributaries feed the river in lowland, it is likely to flood across the floodplain, particularly in winter. When the floods subside, a fine layer of **silt** or **alluvium** is left on the floodplain making this land very fertile and therefore excellent for farming.

Meanders
A meander is a bend in a river. The cross section of a meander (Fig. 2.2.5 below) shows that the water flows faster on the outside of the bend and slower on the inside. This is due to a difference in friction in shallow and deep water. Lateral erosion therefore occurs on the outer bend, and in lowland abrasion and corrosion usually occur, causing the formation of a **river cliff** on the outer bank. On the inside bend the opposite occurs. The water is flowing slowly here and therefore has less energy, resulting in deposition of the river's load. This deposited material builds up to create a **slip-off slope** on the inner bank.

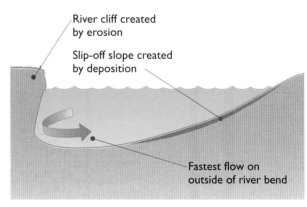

River cliff created by erosion

Slip-off slope created by deposition

Fastest flow on outside of river bend

Fig. 2.2.5: Cross section of a meander

Ox-bow lakes
A river becomes more **sinuous** (has more curves and turns) as it approaches the sea, and meanders may begin to overlap one another. When the necks of the meanders meet each other the river water will take the easiest path downstream and cease to flow around the redundant meander, forming an **ox-bow lake** (Fig. 2.2.6 page 47). As soon as the river water stops flowing in the ox-bow lake, any load, including very fine particles of silt held in suspension, will be deposited. Evaporation will follow and, over time, the redundant meander will be invaded by plant life.

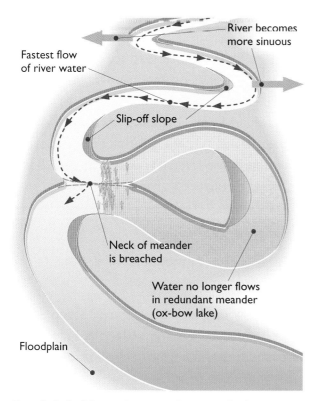

Fig. 2.2.6: Meanders in the river's floodplain leading to ox-bow lakes

Fig. 2.2.7: Aerial photograph showing the lower reaches of a river with a meander and ox-bow lake in the floodplain

Exam tip

Often you will be asked to identify a river feature from the map extract provided with the exam paper. Start by identifying from the contour lines on the map whether it is in highland or lowland and then try to find examples of waterfalls and V-shaped valleys in highland, and meanders and ox-bow lakes in lowland. Look at the map extract of Kirkby Lonsdale on page 65. The contour lines suggest it is in highland because there are contour lines close together, rising either side of the river. If you look at Leck Beck in grid squares 6578 and 6579 it is clearly flowing through a V-shaped valley.

Summary

As a river flows through its drainage basin from source to mouth it will erode, transport and deposit material.

- In highland, where the river has a lot of energy due to it flowing over steep slopes, it will erode vertically to create V-shaped valleys and waterfalls. In lowland the river widens due to the joining of tributaries and begins to erode laterally, creating meanders.

- The lowland river will become more sinuous as it approaches the sea, creating a wide floodplain and forming ox-bow lakes as meanders join one another.

Exercise 2C

 Level 1

1. Write sentences to explain the meaning of each of the following terms:
   river basin   watershed   vertical erosion   lateral erosion

2. (a) Which three processes lead to the formation of a V-shaped valley?
   (b) Draw a well-labelled diagram to illustrate how a V-shaped valley is formed.

3. Draw a flow chart showing the stages in the formation of a waterfall. Use some of the following terms in your explanation: **resistant rock / less resistant rock / hydraulic action / corrosion / backwall / plunge pool / abrasion / transportation / gorge**

4. (a) What is a floodplain?
   (b) Explain why we might find ox-bow lakes upon a floodplain. Use some of the following terms in your explanation: **gradient / lateral erosion / sinuous / neck / deposition / load / photosynthesis / plant invasion**

Exercise 2D

1. Put the following terms in order of where you would find them in the river basin going from highland to lowland:

 tributary   estuary   delta   source

2. Look at the map extract of Kirkby Lonsdale on page 65. How do you account for the fact that Leck Beck (6477) is relatively straight while the River Greta (6272) meanders?

3. Use the internet to research a waterfall of your choice. Write half a page of information about the waterfall based on your research, telling the reader which country the waterfall is in and any interesting facts you have discovered. Avoid copying; try to use your own words and your own knowledge of waterfalls in your answer.

4. Waterfalls and gorges can be formed due to a variety of landform processes. Discuss, using examples.

2.3 Coastal features

Coastal features created by erosion

The results of erosion within a river can be difficult to see, but the effects of the powerful force of the sea on the ever-changing coastline are often more obvious, for example, wide sweeping **bays** and protruding **headlands** riddled with caves.

The four types of erosion at the coast

These are the same four types of erosion that are at work within a river, so there are no more types of erosion to learn. Let's just look at how they work at the coast.

1. Hydraulic action

This is the sheer force of waves hitting exposed cliffs. Air trapped within tiny cracks in the cliff face will be compressed, forcing the rock to weaken and break up upon repetition. The larger the waves, the stronger the effect of hydraulic action.

2. Abrasion

Just as a river picks up pebbles and throws them against its bed and banks, the sea picks up pebbles from the sea floor and beaches and throws them against exposed cliff faces. This erodes the cliffs at their base, creating a line that is known as a **wave-cut notch**. Cliffs collapse over time due to weathering on their tops and undercutting at their base due to abrasion.

3. Attrition

Pebbles from the sea floor and beach constantly collide with each other, as the action of waves breaking on the shore causes them to move forward and back over one another. Just as the river's load becomes smaller and rounder due to attrition so at the coast pebbles also become smaller and rounder due to attrition, ultimately turning into sand.

4. Corrosion

If the cliffs that form the coastline are made of soft rock they may be gradually dissolved as the seawater spray reacts with the rock after a wave has hit them.

Rock type and fetch

Two factors influence how powerfully the sea will erode the coastline: the rock type of the coastline and the **fetch**.

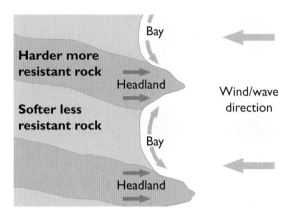

Fig. 2.3.1: Differences in rock type causing headlands and bays

Softer rock such as limestone, sandstone or chalk will erode at a faster rate than harder more resistant rock such as granite. Therefore at a coastline where there is a mixture of different rock types, over thousands of years the different speeds of erosion become evident: headlands are created from the hard rock and bays are eroded from the soft rock between them (Fig. 2.3.1). A good example of this can be seen on the south coast of Britain in Dorset (Fig. 2.3.2 below).

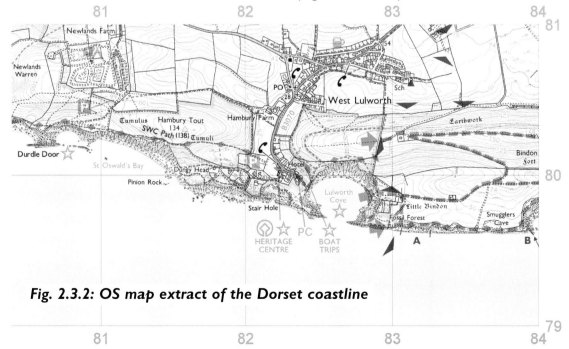

Fig. 2.3.2: OS map extract of the Dorset coastline

Fetch Is the term used to describe how far a wave has to travel before it meets the coastline. The more sea or ocean a wave has to travel across as it is blown by the wind, the larger, and therefore more powerful, it can be. This explains why waves that are blown in by the **prevailing wind** from the Atlantic Ocean tend to be much larger and more powerful than those that break on the east coast of Britain having travelled across the North Sea, a much smaller and shallower stretch of water. The prevailing wind in the UK is from the south west. This is why surfing is better in Cornwall and, along with the variety of rock types in Cornwall, why the coastline there is varied and beautiful.

Headlands and their features

Fig. 2.3.3: Headlands and their features (cracks, caves, arches, stacks and stumps)

Headlands are the hard, resistant outcrops of rock that have taken longer to erode than surrounding softer rock. A headland receives the full force of all four types of erosion as it protrudes out into the sea and receives the waves in deeper water. If the wind direction turns to face the headland side on (Fig. 2.3.3) abrasion will widen cracks at the base of the headland while hydraulic action will widen the crack higher up. Over time the crack will be widened to create a **sea cave**, which in turn will erode through the headland to create an **arch**.

At the same time as the base and sides of the headland are being eroded, weathering will attack the top of the headland. A combination of these two process will lead to the roof of the arch eventually collapsing due to gravity, leaving a **stack**. Abrasion will erode the base of the stack, making it more unstable until it is knocked down, usually in storm conditions by large waves, leaving behind a **stump**.

A very famous example of a headland being shaped in this way can be found on the Dorset coastline near Swanage. The remaining stack has been given the name of Old Harry (Fig. 2.3.4 over the page). The stump that lies before him is called Old Harry's Wife!

Fig. 2.3.4: Old Harry off Swanage in Dorset

Coastal features created by deposition

Beaches

Not all features you see on the coast are created by powerful erosion by waves. Some features are created by the sea depositing material and sometimes it may be a combination of these processes. **Beaches** are created initially by erosion when waves wear away material from the cliff faces they are breaking on. However, this eroded material will be deposited and may eventually build up to create a pebble beach in front of the cliff. These pebbles will be drawn up and down the beach by the action of the waves. Attrition will occur and, depending on the rock type, the pebbles may be worn down to sand.

After erosion of the cliff face the eroded material may be transported along the coastline before being deposited as a beach. This process of transportation is called **longshore drift** and is determined by the

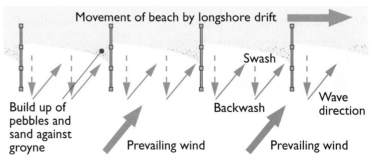

Fig. 2.3.5: Longshore drift

prevailing wind direction. Fig. 2.3.5 (page 52) shows how the waves are blown onto the shore at an angle in the direction of the prevailing wind. Pebbles will be moved by the wave up the beach (swash) at this angle. After the wave has broken it will draw back (backwash) to the sea in a straight line (due to gravity), pulling the pebbles back, before another wave pushes them onto the beach again at an angle. This creates a zig-zag pattern and causes sand and pebbles to be moved along the beach and will also result in attrition.

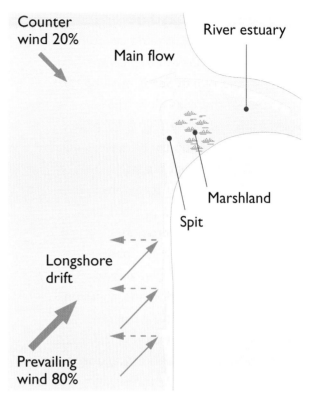

Fig. 2.3.6: The formation of a spit

Spits

A **spit** is a large sandbank that extends along a coastline where there is a change in direction of the land or a river enters the sea (Fig. 2.3.6). Longshore drift transports pebbles and sand along the coast in the direction of the prevailing wind. Shallow water at the end of the coastal stretch reduces the power of the waves so that pebbles and sand are dumped.

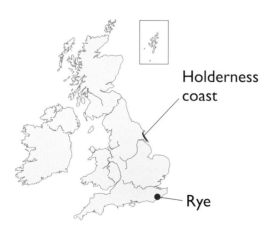

Fig. 2.3.7: Areas of significant coastal erosion and deposition

When this happens at a river mouth river water behind the spit will flow slowly or even stop flowing which results in deposition and the formation of marshland. If the wind blows from the other direction to the prevailing wind for a significant period of time this may force the spit to form a hook on the end. Estuaries do not always have a spit; if the wind direction is not at an angle to the coastline, longshore drift will not occur and therefore a spit will not form at the mouth of the river.

Disappearing coastline

At some points on Britain's coastline erosion is occuring at a rapid rate. For example, the North Sea is eroding the soft rock of the cliffs along the Holderness coastline (Fig. 2.3.7 page 53) at a speed of up to 10 metres per year. This means that coastal settlements are being threatened with falling into the sea! To prevent or at least slow down the erosion, concrete rock armour has been placed at the base of the cliffs to prevent hydraulic action and abrasion eroding and undercutting the cliffs (see Fig. 2.3.8). **Groynes** (Fig. 2.3.5 page 52) have also been used so that

Fig 2.3.8: Concrete rock armour to prevent the erosion of cliffs

pebbles and sand build up to form a beach in front of the cliffs. The beach absorbs wave energy and therefore helps to reduce the wave energy eroding the cliffs.

In other areas of the country deposition is causing new areas of land to be created rather than lost. For example, the town of Rye in East Sussex (Fig. 2.3.7 page 53) was once a port on the coast, but due to deposition is now several miles inland with marshland covering the area where the sea used to be.

Exam tip

Always be sure to distinguish between landform features and landform processes. A feature is something you can see, such as a waterfall in a river or a headland at the coast. A process is the action that may have resulted in the formation of that feature, such as erosion or deposition. Don't get them mixed up!

Summary

The coastline is a very interesting place due to the variety of features we can see and enjoy such as beaches, cliffs and caves. These features are created by processes such as erosion and deposition but are also determined by the rock type that the coastline is made of. Humans have interfered with the natural process of coastal erosion in places such as Holderness to prevent damage to settlements.

Exercise 2E

1. Why do bays appear between headlands along some points of the coastline?

2. Look at grid square 8279 in Fig. 2.3.2 (page 50). Draw a sketch of this grid square and add the following labels:

    headland   bay   soft rock   hard rock

3. Write at least half a page to explain the formation of a cave, an arch, a stack and a stump using and underlining these key words in your answer:

    headland   resistant rock   prevailing wind   hydraulic action
    abrasion   cracks   cave   arch   stack   stump

4. Put the following actions into the correct order to explain how a spit may be formed in a river mouth:

    Slow-moving river water causes deposition and the formation of marshland behind the spit.

    A hook develops on the end of the spit if the wind blows from the opposite direction to the prevailing wind.

    Longshore drift causes pebbles and sand to be moved along the coast in the direction of the prevailing wind.

    Pebbles and sand are deposited in the mouth of the river to create a sandbank called a spit.

5. How do groynes help prevent longshore drift transporting away sand on a beach? Draw a well-labelled diagram to illustrate your answer.

Exercise 2F

1. Explain the meaning of the term 'fetch', referring to areas in Britain where the fetch will vary in significance.

2. On a headland, which types of weathering do you think would assist the collapse of an arch as it is eroded beneath by the sea? Give reasons for your answers.

3. (a) Why is a spit not formed at the mouth of every river?
    (b) Why is there sometimes a hook on the end of a spit?
    (c) What process leads to the formation of marshland behind a spit and why does this make an excellent habitat for birds and other wildlife?

4. Choose one of the statements below and write half a page to discuss your views, referring wherever possible to features, processes and examples. You may also refer to map evidence in Fig. 2.3.2 (page 50).

    The coastline of Britain has always looked the same.

    Nothing can be done to prevent the loss of coastal settlements due to erosion.

2.4 Flooding

Natural disasters are events in nature that have a significant effect on the environment and often lead to human and financial losses. Earthquakes, volcanic eruptions, floods, hurricanes, droughts and landslides are all examples of natural disasters. However, with more and more people living on our planet, many 'natural' disasters may, at least in part, be caused by humans interfering with nature without understanding the consequences.

What causes floods?

When a river can no longer hold all the water it is carrying in its channel it starts to overflow its banks and flood the floodplain either side of it. It is a natural process for rivers to flood; the flooding of floodplains results in the deposition of silt, which makes floodplains fertile and excellent for farming. Flooding is usually caused by very heavy rainfall during winter and spring filling tributaries to a point where the main river overflows. However, it can also be caused by unusually high tides within river estuaries or storms pushing sea water up the river (**storm surges**).

Flash floods occur when the ground cannot absorb water, usually because it has been baked dry in the summer. Flash floods occur after short sharp periods of rainfall and can be devastating. Most floods build up slowly over a number of weeks.

Syllabus example: The Pakistan floods, 2010

Fig. 2.4.1: World map showing Pakistan, the Himalayas and the Indus River

Why Pakistan experiences flooding

Look at Fig. 2.4.1 on page 56. You will see that Pakistan is located at the foot of the western Himalayas. Much of Pakistan therefore receives high levels of river water as a result of annual snowmelt in April and May of each year. However, Pakistan is also subject to a weather system called the monsoon. Monsoon clouds build and continuous pulsating rainfall starts each year in July. This monsoon rainfall usually continues until September, and is important for the economy of the region as it provides rainwater for the crops and is stored and used as drinking water. Tributaries with their sources in the foothills of the Himalayas feed the meltwater from the Himalayas and rainfall received in their river basins from monsoon rain into Pakistan's largest river, the Indus.

Flooding is common on the floodplain of the Indus and occurs every year; however, the 2010 flooding was considerably worse for the following reasons:

- Heavy rainfalls of more than 200 mm (7.9 in) were recorded during the four day wet spell from 27 July to 30 July.

- A record breaking 274 mm (10.8 in) of rain fell in Peshawar during 24 hours. The previous record was 187 mm (7.4 in) of rain in April 2009.

- Monsoon rains were forecasted to continue into early August and were described as the worst in this area in the last 80 years.

- These intense spells of rainfall were falling on **saturated** ground, Therefore, the water was not absorbed and led to flash flooding.

How human activity had increased the risk of flooding

Much of the land that covers the upper parts of the Indus drainage basin has been deforested in order to use the land for agriculture. This deforestation is common in **LEDCs** seeking to improve their level of development. Deforestation, however, increases the amount of rainfall that reaches the river (and therefore can become floodwater) because trees within the drainage basin absorb water through their roots and evaporate it from their leaves (transpiration). Additionally, deforestation results in fine mud (silt) being washed downstream. This silt collects at the bottom of the river's channel in lowland, reducing the amount of water the river can hold and therefore increasing the frequency of flooding.

Another good example of an LEDC in this region that is also unintentionally increasing the risk of flooding due to human activity is Bangladesh. Bangladesh is particularly likely to experience floods because, as well as being at the foot of the Himalayas and experiencing monsoon rainfalls, Bangladesh is extremely low lying and therefore floods easily and can encounter coastal flooding as well.

Immediate effects of the flooding

- An area larger than England was covered in floodwater (approximately 160 000 square kilometres/61 500 square miles)

- Over 20 million people were made homeless as their houses were destroyed by the floodwaters. This is more than the 2004 Indian Ocean tsunami, the 2010 Haiti earthquake and the 2005 Kashmir earthquake combined!

- The Karakoram Highway, which connects Pakistan with China, was closed after a bridge was destroyed.

- In Sindh, the Indus River burst its banks near Sukkur on 8th August, submerging the village of Mor Khan Jatoi. Law and order disappeared, mainly in Sindh. Looters took advantage of the floods to ransack abandoned homes using boats.

- In early August, the heaviest flooding moved southward along the Indus River from severely affected northern regions toward western Punjab, where at least 1 400 000 acres (570 000 ha) of cropland were destroyed.

Now read the media and charity reports (page 60) to find out more information about the immediate effects of the flood. Try to categorise these effects into environmental, economic or social effects.

Longer term effects of the flooding

- In the weeks after the flood 10 million people were forced to drink unsafe drinking water, leading to the spread of water born diseases such as cholera, typhoid and dysentery. On 14th August, the first documented case of cholera emerged in the town of Mingora, striking fear into millions of stranded flood victims. Pakistan also faced a malaria outbreak.

- The economic cost of the flood in terms of lost crops and rebuilding costs to damaged property, roads, etc. is estimated at 43 billion US dollars.

- Floods submerged 69 000 km^2 (26 640 square miles) of Pakistan's most fertile crop land, killed 200 000 livestock and washed away massive amounts of grain. A major concern was that farmers would be unable to meet the autumn deadline for planting new seeds in 2010, which implied a loss of food production in 2011, and potential long term food shortages.

- On 7th September 2010, the International Labour Organization reported that the floods had cost more than 5.3 million jobs. Many families had no savings to draw upon in order to rebuild their lives, and those who did used everything to cover the costs of evacuating their families to safer areas.

Now read the media and charity reports (page 60) to find out more information about the immediate effects of the flood. Try to categorise these effects into environmental, economic or social effects.

How to reduce the risk of flooding

A number of measures can be taken to reduce the risk of flooding occurring in future years. However, to varying degrees, these measures take time and money. Think about which of the methods described below would be appropriate to the Pakistani government following the floods in 2010.

- Building dams and reservoirs on the Indus and its tributaries. Building a dam and flooding a reservoir in the valley behind the dam allows river authorities to control the amount of water going downstream which may result in flooding.

- Planting trees in the river basin of the Indus and its tributaries. This will increase the rate of rainwater absorbed by trees and therefore reduce the amount of water that flows downstream towards the floodplains and cities.

- Creating overflow channels along the course of the river where flooding will be allowed. These are called **diversionary spillways** and allow the river to flood but in a location chosen by man rather than in urban areas.

- Deepening and straightening the river channel. Machinery can be used to dredge the river bed, making it deeper, and the river channel can be made straighter by creating concrete lined banks. Together this will mean the river can hold more water and the water will get to the sea at a faster rate. This should make flooding less likely.

Fig. 2.4.2: Dredging could be used to widen the channel of the Indus River

Media report

Spreading Pakistan floods affect 4m people, says UN: BBC news

"The worst flooding in Pakistan's history has now affected more than four million people and left at least 1600 dead, says the UN."

This report from the BBC continued with a description of how crops, homes, roads and bridges had been washed away, wells had been contaminated and water-borne diseases were spreading. Seven districts in Punjab were reported affected, with 350,000 people moved to neighbouring areas. The BBC report described how:

"Fleeing villagers have waded barefoot through water up to their necks and chests, carrying belongings on their heads. In Punjab, known as Pakistan's 'breadbasket' for its rich agriculture, more than 1300 villages have been affected and at least 25,000 homes destroyed."

Charity report

Oxfam's involvement

On their website, Oxfam reported that they provided humanitarian aid to almost 1.9 million people. This included grants, safe drinking water, sanitation and hygiene facilities, and tents. They also started programs to assist with rebuilding work.

From the general public and institutional sources, Oxfam raised US$62.4 million to support the Pakistan emergency program.

Fig. 2.4.3: Human effects of the Pakistan floods

See also *Geography ISEB Revision Guide* case study on floods.

Exam tip

When asked in the exam about an example of a natural hazard you have studied, such as a river flood, always do the following:

- Name the place where it happened, say which country it occurred in and give the exact date of the event.

- If you are asked about the causes, give detailed facts that you have learnt.

- You may like to explain effects of the natural disaster by splitting them into two groups: immediate effects and long-term effects, and also into natural, human and economic effects.

- Be prepared to discuss how humans have responded to the threat – what they have done to prevent it happening again.

Summary

Natural hazards are disasters where natural forces inflict suffering and destruction upon human beings and their property. Increasingly we are finding that natural disasters occur more often and are made worse by the actions of man. It is vital that, after a natural disaster that has been made worse by humans, local and national authorities learn from the mistakes that have been made in the past.

Exercise 2G

1. What is meant by the term 'natural hazard'? Give some examples.

2. In your own words, explain the meaning of the following terms:
   (a) storm surges
   (b) flash floods

3. (a) Make a star diagram for the 'causes' of the Pakistan floods. Write a title of 'natural' above any cause that was natural and a title of 'human' above any cause that was human.
   (b) Make a star diagram for the 'effects' of the Pakistan floods. Write a title of 'immediate' above any effect that was immediate and a title of 'long-term' above any effect that was long-term.

4. Explain one method that has been adopted to overcome future flooding in Pakistan. You may wish to draw a diagram to support your answer.

5. Look at the map extract of Kirkby Lonsdale on page 65. Give the grid reference of a settlement that may be at risk of flooding. Explain your choice.

Exercise 2H

1. Why is Pakistan always likely to experience flooding?

2. How did human intervention unintentionally increase the flood risk on the Indus?

3. Discuss an advantage and a disadvantage of building dams on the tributaries of the Indus.

Exercise 2I: Enquiry suggestion

You can learn a lot about landform features from books but it is much better to go outside and see them. Not a lot of people are lucky enough to live in the mountains where you can observe V-shaped valleys or waterfalls, or by the coast where you can watch the sea shape the cliffs, headlands and bays. Most of you though are likely to be near a river, so with your teacher or parents you could look at the flow of water within the channel on a straight section of river and on a meander. Use a tape measure and metre ruler to measure the width and depth of the channel. Measure out a 10 metre stretch along the bank. Time how long a cork takes to float along the 10 metre stretch. Using ranging poles at either end of the 10 metre stretch, measure the angle of the river bed with a clinometer (an instrument for measuring angles of slope). Conduct these experiments at different points in the river channel, and compare your results for a straight section of river with results taken on a meander.

Assess whether your river behaves in the way you would expect from what you have learnt.

Exercise 2J: Past exam questions

1. Look at this diagram showing a type of weathering.
   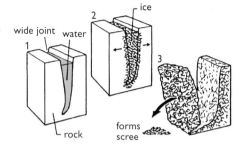
   (a) What is this process called? (1 mark)
   (b) What is the difference between weathering and erosion? (2 marks)
   (c) Copy and complete the table below by putting the following landforms in the correct column to show whether they are formed by erosion or deposition. (4 marks)

   floodplain   stack   waterfall   beach

erosion	deposition

2. With the aid of a labelled diagram or diagrams, explain the formation of a meander. (6 marks)

3. Look at the sketch which shows Hurst Castle spit.
   (a) Make a copy of the sketch and label areas where you would expect erosion, transportation and deposition to take place. (3 marks)
   (b) Explain how the spit has been formed. (5 marks)

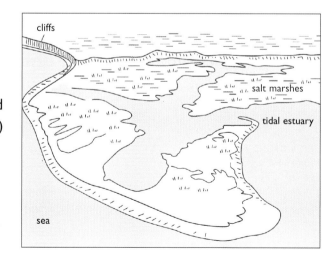

4. Draw a diagram of a waterfall and label it in detail to explain how it was formed. (5 marks)

5. What can be done to prevent flood problems where there is a danger? (4 marks)

Exercise 2K: Scholarship or more advanced question

We all like to be beside the seaside and yet the sea is one of the most dangerous environments known.

(a) What makes the sea a dangerous environment for those living on the coast? (5 marks)

(b) Describe two erosional processes which are at work along the coast. (8 marks)

(c) Why is the coast such a difficult environment to stabilise and control? Use examples to illustrate your answer. (12 marks)

Exercise 2L

Solve the following clues.

1. The action or process of dropping material carried by rivers or the sea (10 letters)
2. A steep-sided valley created after a waterfall or as the result of a collapsed cavern (5 letters)
3. Heaps of broken rock often found on slopes where weathering has taken place (5 letters)
4. An often submerged area of deposited material formed at the mouth of a river (5 letters)
5. A part of the coastline that protrudes into the sea (8 letters)
6. The break up of rock in one place by the weather (10 letters)
7. A stretch of sand or pebbles along the coastline (5 letters)
8. Soil and rock which is waterlogged, causing flooding if there is more rainfall (9 letters)
9. The material carried by a river (4 letters)
10. The wind from the most usual direction (10 letters)

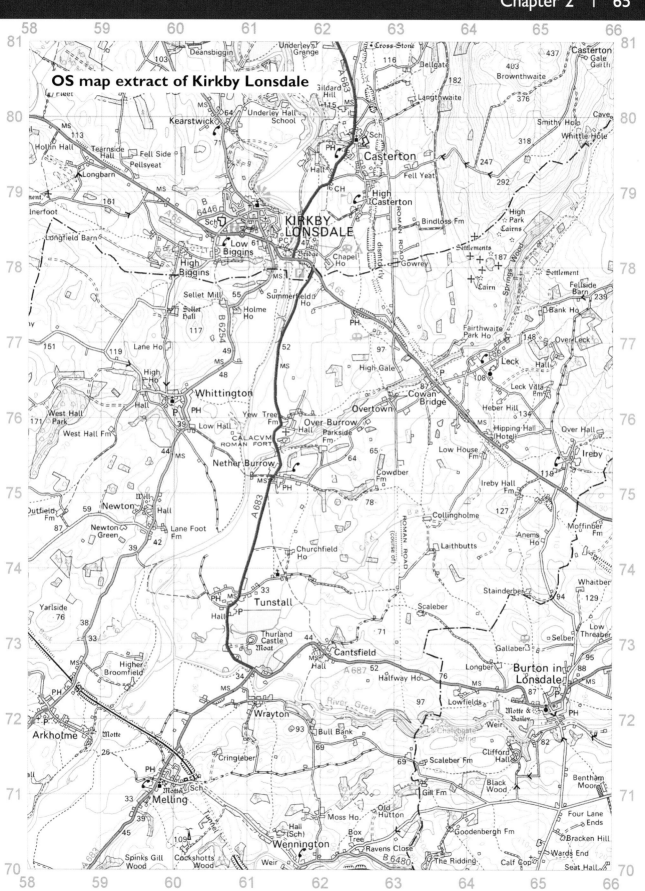

OS map extract of Kirkby Lonsdale

Landform processes glossary

Alluvium	A deposit left by a flooding river.
Arch	A gap created in a coastal headland due to processes of erosion.
Bay	A broad curved inlet to the sea or a lake.
Beach	A stretch of sand or pebbles along the coastline.
Biological weathering	The breakdown of rock by plants and animals.
Channel	The bed and banks of a river within which the water flows.
Chemical weathering	The breakdown of rock by acid in rain and river water.
Confluence	Where a tributary joins the main river.
Delta	An often submerged area of deposited material formed at the mouth of a river.
Deposition	The action or process of dropping material (load) carried by rivers or the sea.
Diversionary spillway	A designated area for river flooding.
Erosion	The wearing away and removal of rock and soil by rivers, sea, ice and wind.
Estuary	Where fresh river water meets the tide and salt water of the sea.
Exfoliation	The breakdown of rock by repeated heating and cooling, causing layers of the rock to peel off. See onion-skin weathering.
Fetch	The distance a wave travels before it breaks on the shore.
Flash floods	Rapid flooding caused by heavy rainfall hitting impermeable surfaces.
Floodplain	The flat land either side of a river which is rich in fertile soil.
Freeze-thaw weathering	The process of weathering where water in cracks freezes, expands and shatters the rock. See frost shattering.
Frost shattering	The process of weathering where water in cracks freezes, expands and shatters the rock. See freeze-thaw weathering.

Gorge	A steep-sided valley created after a waterfall or as the result of a collapsed cavern.
Gradient	The steepness of a slope.
Groynes	Wooden barriers erected along beaches to prevent longshore drift.
Headland	A part of the coastline that protrudes into the sea.
Lateral erosion	Erosion of the sides of a river channel, which occurs in lowland due to the gentle gradient.
LEDC	Less Economically Developed Country.
Load	The material carried by a river.
Longshore drift	The movement of sand and pebbles along a beach in the direction of the prevailing wind.
Mass movement	The movement of weathered soil and rock on a slope.
Meander	A curve or bend in a river commonly found in lowland.
Mouth	The end of a river where it reaches the sea or a lake.
Natural disaster	Events where natural forces have a significant effect on the enviroment, human beings and their property.
Onion-skin weathering	The breakdown of rock by repeated heating and cooling causing layers of the rock to peel off like the skin of an onion. See exfoliation.
Ox-bow lake	Redundant meander which occurs in lowland where the banks of a meander have joined and river water has taken the fastest route downstream.
Plunge pool	A depression at the bottom of a waterfall caused by hydraulic action.
Prevailing wind	The dominant wind direction.
Rapid	Uneven river bed leading to white water.
River basin	An area of land drained by a river and its tributaries.

River cliff	The steeper outside bank of the river undercut by the fastest flowing water.
Saturated	Waterlogged. When soil or rock is saturated, further rainfall causes flooding.
Scree	Heaps of broken rock often found on slopes where weathering has taken place.
Sea cave	A cave carved out of a headland due to erosion by the sea.
Silt	The fine material carried by a river.
Sinuous	Having many curves and turns.
Slip-off slope	The gentle slope formed by deposition on the inside of a river meander.
Source	The beginning of a river in highland such as a glacier or a spring.
Spit	A narrow stretch of sand and shingle that protrudes from the shoreline into the mouth of a river.
Spur	Valley side in highland.
Stack	An outcrop of rock in the sea just off the coast, created by erosion of the headland.
Storm surge	Unusually high tide sweeping up a river estuary caused by a storm out at sea and resulting in flooding.
Stump	The remains of a stack that has been knocked over.
Temperature range	The difference between minimum and maximum temperature in a 24-hour period.
Transportation	The movement of a river's load downstream.
Tributary	A small river which joins a bigger river.
Vertical erosion	Erosion downwards into the rock which occurs in highland due to the steep gradient.
V-shaped valley	A steep-sided valley found in highland and created by weathering and erosion.

Waterfall	A steep step or fall in the gradient of a river and found in highland.
Watershed	The dividing line between two or more river basins.
Wave-cut notch	A deep indent running along the base of a cliff, caused by the force of the waves undercutting the rock.
Weathering	The break up of rock by the weather and biological agents.

Chapter 3: Weather and climate

Meteorologist forecasting the weather

Damage caused by a hurricane

Climate change affects all life

In this chapter we will look at:

- How variations in the atmosphere are driven by the global water cycle.

- What is weather and what is climate.

- The causes of temperature and rainfall variations over a small area such as your school grounds.

- What Britain's climate is like and what causes it to be like it is.

- A very different climate along the equator.

- The different weather systems that affect Britain and the three different types of rainfall we can receive in Britain.

- Why we should be worried about climate change and what it is like to be caught in a hurricane!

3.1 What is weather and what is climate?

The difference between weather and climate

Candidates in Geography exams are often asked to define the difference between weather and climate. There are three differences:

Weather is the atmospheric conditions (temperature, precipitation, wind speed and direction, air pressure) which can change over a very short period of time (a few hours) and a short distance (a few miles).

Climate is defined as the weather averaged over long periods of time. Climate can be defined by measures such as temperature and rainfall. It takes many years for any change in climate to occur and you have to travel thousands of miles before you enter a different climatic region.

Measuring the weather

There is a lot of attention from the media at the moment upon climate change and its consequences. We must appreciate that in reality any significant climate change takes many years to occur. However, living in Britain you cannot have missed the fact that the weather rarely stays the same for very long, perhaps explaining why the British are well known for always talking about the weather! Look at the climate graph of Bishop's Stortford (Fig. 3.1.1). This climate graph will vary very little from year to year but if we

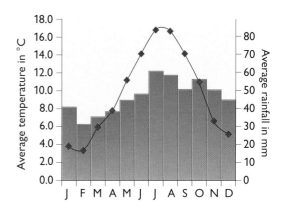

Fig. 3.1.1: Climate graph for Bishop's Stortford

observed the weather forecast for Bishop's Stortford's region we would notice the weather changing from day to day, if not hour to hour.

Many people rely on accurate weather forecasts to plan and prepare aspects of their lives. Fishermen need to know the sea conditions before setting sail, farmers make important decisions concerning their crop based on the weather and organisers of major sporting events need accurate information. Of course we all want to know what the weather will be like for our leisure time at the weekend, especially if it involves being outdoors.

The scientists who measure the weather and give information for weather forecasts are known as **meteorologists**. Meteorologists focus mainly on four aspects of the weather:

- wind speed and direction
- temperature in the soil and in the air
- amount of precipitation and moisture in the air
- air pressure.

An **anemometer** is used to measure wind speed and is combined with a wind vane to determine the direction from which the wind is coming. Look at Fig. 3.1.2 (below) to find the symbol used to represent wind speed and direction on weather maps. You may see these in newspapers or on television weather forecasts.

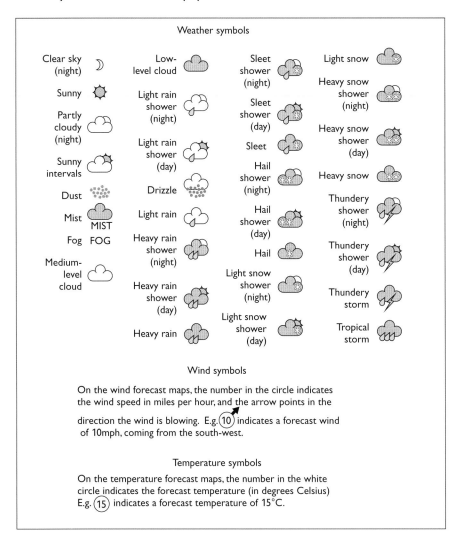

Fig. 3.1.2: Typical symbols used on a weather map

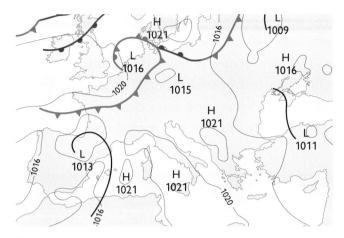

Fig. 3.1.3: A weather map of Europe

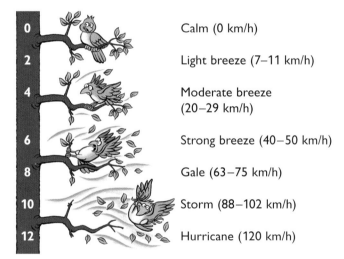

0	Calm (0 km/h)
2	Light breeze (7–11 km/h)
4	Moderate breeze (20–29 km/h)
6	Strong breeze (40–50 km/h)
8	Gale (63–75 km/h)
10	Storm (88–102 km/h)
12	Hurricane (120 km/h)

Fig. 3.1.4: The Beaufort scale

Fig. 3.1.6: A rain gauge

Air pressure is represented on weather maps by thin black lines of equal air pressure called **isobars** (see Fig. 3.1.3 left).

The closer the isobars are on the weather map, the windier the weather. The **Beaufort scale** (see Fig. 3.1.4 below) categorises wind by speed and the level of damage the wind can cause. A maximum/minimum thermometer (see Fig. 3.1.5) is used to measure the **temperature range** over a 24-hour period. A **rain gauge** (see Fig. 3.1.6) collects precipitation which is measured in millimetres.

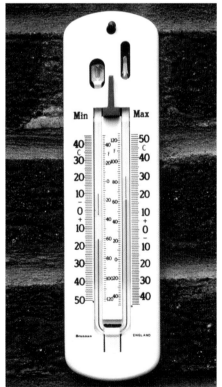

Fig. 3.1.5: A maximum/minimum thermometer

A **barometer** (see Fig. 3.1.7) measures the air pressure in units called millibars. The important middle point is 1000 mb, with 940 mb indicating very stormy weather and 1050 mb very fine weather. When the air pressure is falling this means that winds will increase, bringing more cloud cover and possibly rainfall. When air pressure is rising this means winds will become lighter and skies clearer, giving sunshine. In this way, meteorologists can not only observe and record the weather but also vitally predict it.

Fig. 3.1.7: A barometer

Technology is increasingly being used to observe, measure, model and predict the weather these days. However, you may well find all the instruments mentioned above stored in a weather station called a **Stevenson screen** located within your school grounds (Fig. 3.1.8 right).

Fig. 3.1.8: A Stevenson screen

Air masses

One of the reasons why Britain experiences ever-changing weather patterns is that we are in an unusual geographical position where we are affected by five **air masses**. An air mass is a large body of air stretching hundreds of miles in length and width, all of which has a similar level of moisture and temperature properties. The air mass gets its moisture and temperature from its source regions which are usually flat areas of water or land. Air masses are defined by their origin and the course they travel.

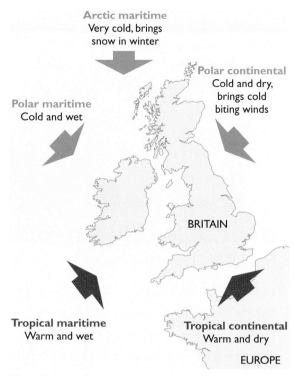

Look at Fig. 3.1.9. The reason why we receive so much rainfall in Britain is because over 80% of the time the wind

Fig. 3.1.9: Air masses influencing Britain

blows from the south-west, bringing the tropical maritime air mass over Britain. This **prevailing wind** from the south-west means that most of the time the air over Britain has travelled over the ocean and therefore contains a lot of moisture which is deposited firstly on Ireland, and then on Britain. When on rare occasions the wind blows from the south we are lucky enough to receive the tropical continental air mass which will be dry and warm as it has travelled largely over land, not sea, from Northern Africa. A northerly or easterly wind in winter will often result in very cold snowy conditions generated from the arctic maritime or polar continental air masses. Winds from the north-west receive the cold wet weather of the polar maritime air mass.

The water cycle

In order to understand all aspects of the weather, we first need to understand the engine that drives the weather within our **atmosphere**. This engine is called the **water cycle** or the **hydrological cycle**. There is a finite amount of water in the world. Some water is stored as ice at the North and South Poles, some water is held within the atmosphere in clouds, water flows over the land as rivers and of course two thirds of the earth's surface is covered by oceans. Within the water cycle, water moves from one area of storage or state to another. Such movements between water stores are called **transfers**.

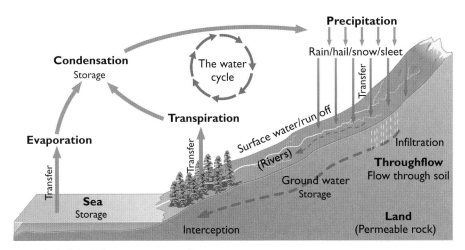

Fig. 3.1.10: The water cycle

Look at Fig. 3.1.10 above. The water cycle begins with water being transferred from the sea into the atmosphere, a process called **evaporation**. The heat of the sun causes water particles in the ocean to become a gas which we call **water vapour** and rise up into the atmosphere. At the same time **transpiration** will occur. Transpiration is the transfer of water from the leaves of trees into the atmosphere upon heating by the sun. Through their roots, trees absorb or **intercept** water that is in the soil or rock below them.

As water vapour rises through the atmosphere following evaporation and transpiration it begins to cool. The temperature falls by approximately 1°C for every 100 metres you ascend. That is why it is always cold on the top of high mountains, even in summer. As the water vapour cools, the water particles in the air move closer together and can be seen as clouds, a process called **condensation**. Winds blow the clouds further inland, causing them to rise over higher land and consequently cool further. If the water particles contract enough they will reform as water droplets and begin to fall as either rain, hail, snow or sleet depending on the atmosphere temperature. This process is called **precipitation**.

The water cycle is completed when precipitation returns to the sea. It flows overland as rivers or, depending on the rock type, gradually seeps through the rock back to rivers or the sea. This only occurs if the rock is **permeable**, meaning it acts like a sponge and allows water to pass through it. Water moving through rocks is called **throughflow** and can then be stored in the rock as **groundwater**, or it can pass through to the sea. Of course, groundwater may be intercepted by trees and transpired before it has a chance to reach any rivers or the sea.

Microclimate

Microclimate is the term that describes slight changes in temperature and precipitation within a small area. You may well have felt changes in temperature or gusts of wind that make you feel cold around your school grounds but never really thought about what causes these differences. These changes in temperature and rainfall can be caused by different factors (Fig. 3.1.11).

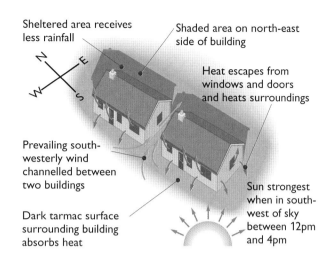

Sheltered area receives less rainfall

Shaded area on north-east side of building

Heat escapes from windows and doors and heats surroundings

Prevailing south-westerly wind channelled between two buildings

Dark tarmac surface surrounding building absorbs heat

Sun strongest when in south-west of sky between 12pm and 4pm

Fig. 3.1.11: The different ways a building can influence microclimate

Shelter

If you hide behind a wall or a building on a windy day, you are taking shelter to keep warm. It will feel a degree or two warmer on the sheltered side of the wall or building than on the side facing the wind. Buildings, walls, hills, valleys and many other features can provide shelter. Often the wind blows from the same direction (prevailing wind) so the same feature can regularly provide shelter.

Surface

Dark surfaces absorb heat and therefore are warmer than light shiny surfaces. The Sun's heat will be absorbed by dark surfaces such as tarmac and will radiate from it, increasing the temperature. This is why when it rains in the summer you can often see the water evaporate immediately on tarmac surfaces but not on lighter surfaces like grass.

Aspect

The **aspect** of a slope describes the direction in which it faces. As the sun moves through the sky, it warms those slopes that are facing it. In Britain the sun rises in the east and moves through the south before setting in the west. This means that south-facing slopes receive more sun than north-facing slopes. Houses in Britain that have south-facing gardens fetch more money than houses with colder north-facing gardens.

Buildings

Other than acting as shelter and blocking out sunlight, buildings have two main effects on microclimate. During the day dark buildings absorb heat from the sun. They radiate it out, making the surrounding area a degree or two warmer. This effect is amplified in winter when buildings have central heating in them and it is colder outside. Buildings also break up or funnel the wind depending on the direction they are facing and the prevailing wind direction. You will often find temperatures in cities are slightly higher than in the surrounding countryside.

Natural physical features

Trees are a good example of natural shelter. Rain is caught in the canopy of a forest, reducing precipitation. In winter, it feels warmer in a sheltered forest as the trees provide protection from the cooling wind. In summer it feels cooler, as the trees provide protection from the Sun. Areas of water such as lakes and the sea have a cooling effect on the land adjoining them and can produce cooling breezes.

Exam tip

It is very easy to confuse different terms in Geography. Don't confuse weather with weathering. Weather is the observation of the atmospheric conditions whereas weathering, discussed in Chapter 2, is the breakdown of rock by the weather. Often candidates confuse transpiration with transportation. Transpiration is a transfer within the water cycle in which water is evaporated from the leaves of trees whereas transportation, again discussed in Chapter 2, is the movement of material, for example, by rivers or the sea. Use the glossary at the end of each chapter to make sure you understand and can define the geographical terms associated with each topic.

Summary

Weather is what we experience on a daily basis. When weather is averaged over months and years we can create a generalised view of two key aspects of our weather, the temperature and rainfall, which we call climate. Weather is observed by meteorologists who use their knowledge of air masses to predict the weather we will receive depending on the wind direction. Smaller scale shifts in temperature and rainfall would not be detailed on a weather forecast but these differences in microclimate are considered when designing and constructing new buildings.

Exercise 3A

1. Draw two spider diagrams to summarise the difference between weather and climate (see page 40 to remind yourself of what a spider diagram is if you have forgotten).

2. What is a Stevenson screen? Describe what equipment you may find in a Stevenson screen and what it would measure.

3. Why does Britain receive a lot of rainfall? Discuss the **prevailing wind** and **air masses** in your answer.

4. Write a sentence to explain the meaning of each of the following terms as they are used within the water cycle:
   (a) evaporation
   (b) transpiration
   (c) condensation
   (d) precipitation

5. What is microclimate? How do buildings affect microclimate? Use the following terms in your answer:
   aspect   shade   shelter   prevailing wind
   wind channelling   winter   surface

 Exercise 3B

1. If the isobars are spread well apart from each other on a weather map, what do you think the weather would be like and which air mass or air masses do you think would be influencing Britain?

2. '**Permeable** rock allows increased **interception** and therefore more transpiration.'

   Explain this statement making sure you define the terms in bold within your answer.

3. Write at least half a page to explain how different features on your school campus, both man-made (e.g. buildings) and natural (e.g. trees), influence the microclimate. You may use illustrations to complement your answer.

4. Why are the British people always talking, and complaining, about the weather?

3.2 Contrasting climates

Global climate bands

Very broadly speaking we can split the world up into different bands of climate that stretch across the globe by **latitude**. Lines of latitude are the imaginary lines that run horizontally around the globe. As you move towards higher latitudes nearing the North and South Poles the climate becomes significantly colder. Likewise, as you move towards lower latitudes nearing the Equator the climate becomes hotter. Whether the climate is wet or dry usually depends on the amount of ocean surrounding the land and if the prevailing wind is blowing from the ocean.

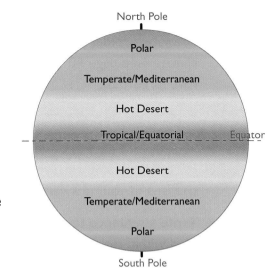

Fig. 3.2.1: Generalised climate bands by latitude

In this way we find similar climate bands spread across similar latitudes on either side of the Equator (Fig. 3.2.1). For example, the climate in Britain is similar to the climate of Western Canada and New Zealand because they are all approximately the same distance from the Equator, they are all close to major oceans and all receive the prevailing wind from the sea.

Temperate maritime climate of the British Isles

The climate of the Britsh Isles is described as **temperate maritime**, which means that Britain generally experiences warm summers and mild winters due to its location at the edge of the European continent, with rainfall occurring throughout the year.

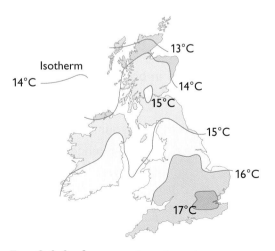

Fig. 3.2.2: Average temperatures in British Isles for July

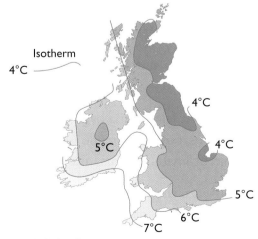

Fig. 3.2.3: Average temperatures in British Isles for January

This is evident from the climate graph of Bishop's Stortford shown on page 71. As well as being displayed on a climate graph the climate can be illustrated on maps that indicate the average temperature and average amount of precipitation received across the country. Look at Figs. 3.2.2, 3.2.3 and 3.2.4. Each shows different information. Figs. 3.2.2 and 3.2.3 indicate how average temperature varies over the British Isles in July and January, summer and winter. A pattern is created by the blue lines that link areas of equal temperature; these are called **isotherms**. Do you notice any difference in the pattern created by the isotherms between Figs. 3.2.2 and 3.2.3? Fig. 3.2.4 shows how much annual precipitation is received across Britain. Which areas of Britain receive most rainfall?

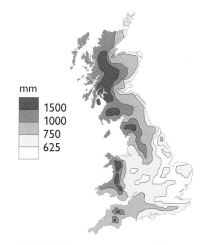

Fig. 3.2.4: Average annual precipitation in Britain

Factors affecting the climate of the British Isles
There are five factors that work together to create these patterns of temperature and precipitation and influence our climate, making it temperate.

1. Latitude
If you watch the weather forecast you will notice that often it is warmer in the south than in the north of Britain (Fig. 3.2.2 on page 80). This is because the Sun's rays have further to travel through our atmosphere to reach the north of Britain and are entering the atmosphere at a wider angle. The atmosphere contains a layer of ozone that filters out the power of the Sun. Rays that travel further north have more ozone to pass through, making them weaker (Fig. 3.2.5). This is why it gets colder as you move towards the Poles and hotter as you move towards the Equator.

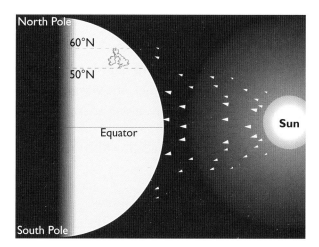

Fig. 3.2.5: How latitude influences the climate of the British Isles

2. The Gulf Stream

Fig. 3.2.3 (page 80) shows that, as well as being warmer in the south than the north, it is also warmer in the west and cooler in the east. This pattern is created by the warming influence of the **Gulf Stream** (**North Atlantic Drift**), a current of warm water that flows from the Gulf of Mexico along the south-west coast of Britain. This effect is most influential in the winter months.

3. South-westerly prevailing winds

Look again at the map of the air masses influencing Britain (page 75). The arrow to the south-west represent the prevailing wind that blows 80% of the time. This wind travels over thousands of miles of Atlantic Ocean and it picks up a lot of moisture ready to drop it on the first landmass it meets, which is Ireland and Britain. Both the polar maritime and the tropical maritime air masses carry a lot of water vapour. This explains why the west of Britain has more rainfall than the east.

4. Altitude

Altitude describes the height of the land. In Britain most of the mountainous or very hilly areas are in the west (e.g. Snowdonia in Wales) or in the north (e.g. the Pennines in northern England or the North West Highlands in Scotland). For every 100 metres you ascend, it gets 1°C cooler, so northern and western areas of Britain are generally colder. Condensation and precipitation occur over highland causing the north and the west to be wetter than other areas of Britain (Fig. 3.2.4 page 81).

5. Distance from the sea

As the land warms more quickly than the sea, and also cools more quickly, coastal areas can be cooler in summer but warmer in winter. As with the warming Gulf Stream, the influence of the sea in raising coastal temperatures is most noticeable in winter.

Singapore's equatorial climate – syllabus extra/scholarship

Fig. 3.2.6: South East Asia   *Fig. 3.2.7: Singapore*

Singapore is a very small country that is situated at the end of the Malayan **peninsula**. Unlike many of the regions that surround it, Singapore has become a wealthy republic due to its port that services trading routes across the South China Sea. Over four million people live in Singapore, many of whom are British businessmen and women working in the country for a number of years. It is these people who are most likely to notice the clear contrast between Singapore's **equatorial climate** and Britain's temperate climate.

A close analysis of Fig. 3.2.8 reveals that there are no seasons in Singapore, with temperatures remaining high all year round and rain falling throughout the year. Rainfall levels are much higher in Singapore than in Britain. This rain, combined with the constantly high temperatures, produces a very high level of **humidity**, making the air feel sticky. Each day is very similar, starting with clear skies and sunshine but leading to cloudy afternoons often punctuated by heavy thunderstorms later in the afternoon.

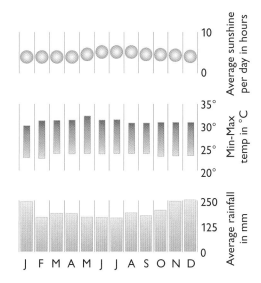

Fig. 3.2.8: Climate graph for Singapore

Factors affecting Singapore's climate

Three principal factors influence Singapore's equatorial climate:

1. Latitude

If you look at Fig. 3.2.6 (page 82) again you will notice that Singapore lies only 2° north of the Equator. This means that whatever time of the year it is, Singapore always receives direct overhead Sun which heats the land and surrounding sea. This is why the monthly temperature never fluctuates significantly.

2. Surrounding sea

Singapore is at the very end of a peninsula protruding into the South China Sea and is surrounded by water on all sides. This has two effects on the climate. Firstly, the sea warms the land throughout the year, acting like a hot water bottle at the foot of the peninsula. The direct overhead Sun heats the sea water surrounding Singapore, as it does the land, but the sea water holds its temperature longer than land, therefore providing an insulating effect at night. Secondly, the surrounding sea is responsible for the high levels of precipitation that Singapore receives throughout the year. This is because direct overhead Sun leads to high levels of evaporation and condensation which is released over the land as **convectional rainfall** (see page 89).

3. Prevailing winds

If you look closely at Fig. 3.2.8 (page 83) you will notice that rainfall is slightly higher in the period between November and January. This is a result of **monsoon** winds which blow from high pressure in northern Asia to low pressure in northern Australia at this time of the year. This adds to the convectional rain that falls throughout the year.

Comparing the climates of the British Isles and Singapore

Singapore's annual average temperature is 30°C compared to a cooler annual average temperature in Britain of just 10°C. This clear difference in temperature is a result of the difference in latitude between Singapore, which has a latitude of 2° north, and Britain which has a latitude between 50° and 60° north. Temperatures vary much more in Britain than Singapore both throughout the year and from place to place. Factors such as relief and location in relation to the five air masses are responsible for regional variations in temperature within Britain. The Gulf Stream, a warm and powerful ocean current, carries warm water across the Atlantic and also makes winters in Western Europe warmer than they would otherwise be.

The surrounding sea and effect of the monsoon winds gives Singapore a total annual rainfall of 2357 mm. Britain's temperate climate gives us a total annual rainfall of around 1350 mm, considerably less than Singapore. Again a much higher degree of regional variation in precipitation is experienced in Britain due to relief and location in relation to the south-westerly prevailing winds.

Exam tip

If you are asked to interpret a climate graph or a map showing differences across Britain of temperature or rainfall always quote specific information. For example, if asked to interpret Fig. 3.2.3 (page 80) you should say what the temperature is in which region and what pattern is evident, for example: 'Fig. 3.2.3 shows average temperatures across Britain in January. You can see that the average temperature increases as you move towards the south-west of Britain where the average January temperature is 7°C compared to just 4°C in the north-east of Britain.'

Summary

Generally we find that climate changes with latitude, producing climate bands that are found in both the northern and southern hemisphere. Britain's climate is a temperate climate, meaning it experiences warm summers and winters with rainfall occurring throughout the year. This pattern is created by factors such as Britain's latitude, the relief of the land, the effect of the Gulf Stream and the influence of our prevailing south-westerly winds. Singapore experiences the very different equatorial climate which gives a hot and humid feel to the weather throughout the year.

Level 1

Exercise 3C

1. (a) What is the word used to describe Britain's climate?
    (b) Write a sentence to describe what Britain's climate is like.
    (c) Why do we find temperate climates in areas of the globe far away from Britain such as New Zealand?

2. Explain why it is warmer in the south of Britain than the north of Britain in July.

3. (a) Describe what Fig. 3.2.3 (page 80) shows. Use directions in your answer and quote figures from the map.
    (b) If you decided to go for a swim in the sea on Christmas Day which coast would be warmest? Explain your choice.

4. Why is it drier in the east of Britain than the west? Use the following terms in your answer:
    prevailing wind   air masses

5. (a) What is the word used to describe Singapore's climate?
    (b) Draw a star diagram to summarise the three factors that influence Singapore's climate. In the centre of your star diagram write 'Singapore's equatorial climate' and underneath write a short sentence to describe the climate.

Level 2

Exercise 3D

1. Why are the coldest and wettest places in Britain often the same place? Refer to Fig. 3.2.4 (page 81) in your answer and mention specific places.

2. What is humidity and why is humidity so high in Singapore?

3. Although Britain and Singapore have very different climates, both climates are heavily influenced by the sea. Explain the role of the sea in creating these climates.

3.3 Weather systems and the rain they bring to Britain

Anticyclones and depressions – syllabus extra/scholarship

We all know that the British weather can be very changeable; one day it can be warm and sunny and the next it can be cool and wet. As we have already learnt, air masses are partially responsible for these variations. Britain also experiences two different types of weather systems: anticyclones and depressions. These represent variations in air pressure and lead to contrasting weather conditions on the ground.

Fig. 3.3.1: Weather associated with anticyclones and depressions

Weather system	Anticyclones	Depressions
Process	Cool air sinking	Warm air rising
Airmasses	One airmass – usually polar continental in winter; tropical continental in summer	Two airmasses – usually tropical maritime rising over polar maritime
Isobars on map	Isobars dispersed	Isobars tightly packed
Weather	Still or very light winds; clear skies and sunny; no rainfall	Windy; cloudy skies with no sun; frontal rainfall
Seasonal variation	Very cold in winter (sometimes foggy); very hot in summer	Wet, mild and windy throughout the year
Pressure	High pressure	Low pressure

An **anticyclone** is a high pressure weather system. This is indicated on a weather map by dispersed isobars. This high pressure is created by the cool dry air of an anticyclone sinking to the ground. As the air slowly sinks it warms, evaporating any cloud. Anticyclones therefore always give clear skies which makes the temperature very cold in winter and very hot in summer. Whatever the time of year, anticyclones are always associated with light winds and calm stable weather. Pressure is measured in millibars; 1050 mb is high pressure.

Depressions are low pressure weather systems created when cold and warm air masses meet. Due to the prevailing south-westerly wind in Britain, the tropical

Fig. 3.3.2: Satellite image of a depression (white swirl of cloud) over the Atlantic Ocean

maritime and polar maritime air masses often meet to form depressions in the Atlantic Ocean to the west of Britain and Ireland (see Fig. 3.3.2). When these two air masses meet they do not mix due to their different temperatures. The warm (tropical maritime) air mass is forced to rise over the cooler (polar maritime) air mass at a boundary known as a **front**. As the air rises it cools, condenses and precipitates along the front; this results in a type of rainfall known as **frontal rainfall**. As the depression moves from the Atlantic over Britain, two fronts will sweep over the country giving us mild but wet and windy conditions. Depressions are more likely in winter but can occur at any time of the year. Low pressure would give a reading of 940 mb.

The three types of rainfall which Britain receives

If you have ever returned to Britain from a holiday abroad one of the first things you are likely to notice is how green Britain's countryside is. This is because we receive a higher amount of rainfall than our European neighbours. The amount of rainfall a place within Britain receives depends on where it is located in the country because this determines which type or types of rainfall it receives: frontal, relief or convectional rainfall.

Although we say there are three types of rainfall, the process that creates rainfall (precipitation) is always the same. Remember that air cools by around 1°C for every 100 metres it rises in the atmosphere. Chilled water vapour condenses into clouds. When clouds are forced to rise even further in the atmosphere the water vapour reforms as water droplets and falls as rain, or snow, hail or sleet if it is cold enough.

1. Relief rainfall

Relief is the geographical term that describes the height of the land. Mountains or hills are *the cause* of air rising in **relief rainfall**, leading to *the process* described above. Most of the mountain ranges in Britain lie in the north and west of the country such as the North West Highlands in Scotland, Snowdonia in Wales and the Lake District in Cumbria.

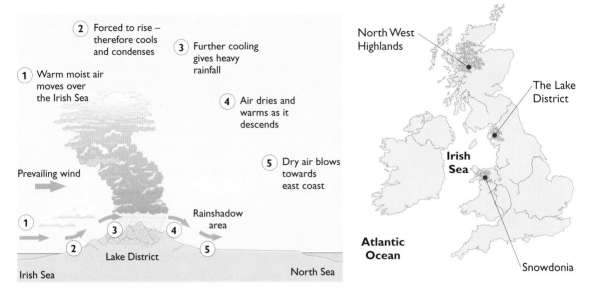

Fig. 3.3.3: Relief rainfall in the Lake District

Fig. 3.3.4: Map of Britain highlighting location of the Lake District

Look at the figures above. Prevailing south-westerly winds, generated from the tropical maritime and polar maritime air masses meeting, blow moist air towards the Lake District from the Atlantic Ocean. Some rain will be deposited over the hills of Ireland but the winds will regain moisture over the Irish Sea before meeting the coast and mountains of the Lake District. Only a few miles inland, these moist winds are suddenly forced to rise over mountains nearly 1000 m (3200 ft) high. This causes very rapid condensation then precipitation. After the rainfall has been released, the air descends, warms and dries over an area to the east of the mountains known as the **rainshadow**. Most settlements in the Lake District are located in the eastern part of the mountains as this area receives considerably less rainfall.

2. Frontal rainfall

Britain's prevailing south-westerly winds cause the polar maritime and tropical maritime air masses to meet over the Atlantic Ocean and create depressions. Where two air masses of different temperatures meet, a boundary called a front is formed. The two air masses do not mix due to their difference in temperature. The warm air mass

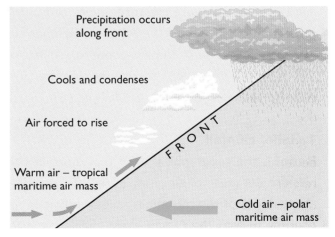

Fig. 3.3.5: Frontal rainfall

rises over the cold air mass. The air cools by around 1°C for every 100 metres it rises. Condensation and precipitation then occur (see Fig. 3.3.5 page 88). A depression has two fronts which, as they sweep across Britain, give two periods of rainfall that can last several hours. Frontal rainfall often begins in the north-west of Britain but usually spreads across all areas. Depressions and the frontal rainfall they bring are more common in winter but can occur at any time of the year.

Fig. 3.3.6: Convectional rainfall – a thunderstorm

3. Convectional rainfall

Fig. 3.3.6 shows a typical thunderstorm that may occur at the end of an extremely hot day in Britain. Convectional rainfall occurs with thunderstorms and is caused by the sun evaporating large amounts of water from the Earth's surface on a very hot day. Water is evaporated from trees (transpiration), rivers, lakes and the sea. Warm air rising from the ground pushes condensed clouds higher and higher in the atmosphere until they quickly cool and suddenly release their moisture in violent and heavy downpours of rain.

Convectional rainfall is often accompanied by lightning, which is created by the rapid evaporation of water vapour generating an electrical charge. Convectional rainfall is rare in Britain as the sun is usually not out for long enough to cause sufficient levels of evaporation. Convectional rainfall however is common in equatorial climates which receive direct overhead Sun and are surrounded by the sea or large river basins such as the Amazon.

Exam tip

If you are given the choice of which type of rainfall to explain in the exam, it would be a good idea to choose relief rainfall. This type of rainfall is the easiest to remember because it is the one which is most similar to the water cycle, and an easy example to refer to would be the Lake District. If you draw a diagram to support your answer, don't forget to include detailed labels highlighting features such as the prevailing south-westerly winds and the rainshadow area.

Summary

The weather Britain receives is related to the weather system it is experiencing:

- Low pressure weather systems are called depressions and bring mild, wet and windy weather at any time of the year.

- Anticyclones are high pressure weather systems which bring us still, clear weather with high temperatures in summer and cold icy conditions in winter.

Depressions give rise to frontal rainfall which can occur anywhere in Britain. Relief rainfall is confined to the mountainous north-west of Britain, while convectional rainfall only occurs in isolated areas following very hot days.

Exercise 3E

1. Look at the map extract of Cockermouth on the next page. Study the map and find out where Cockermouth is in Britain.
   (a) What type of rainfall do you think Cockermouth may receive on a regular basis? Give reasons for your choice.
   (b) Look at grid square 1931. On a hot day in August what type of rainfall do you think the hamlet of Dubwath may receive? Give reasons for your choice.
   (c) Some areas of Britain receive all three types of rainfall. Is Cockermouth one of these places? Give reasons for your answer.

2. Why does the Lake District receive so much rainfall? Use the following words in your answer:
   prevailing south-westerly winds   condensation   rainshadow

3. Create a flow chart to explain what happens in the process of frontal rainfall. Begin with a box that says:

   Warm and cold air masses meet in Atlantic Ocean

4. Create a diagram to explain convectional rainfall. Make sure you add detailed labels to your diagram mentioning why the air is forced to rise and what causes lightning.

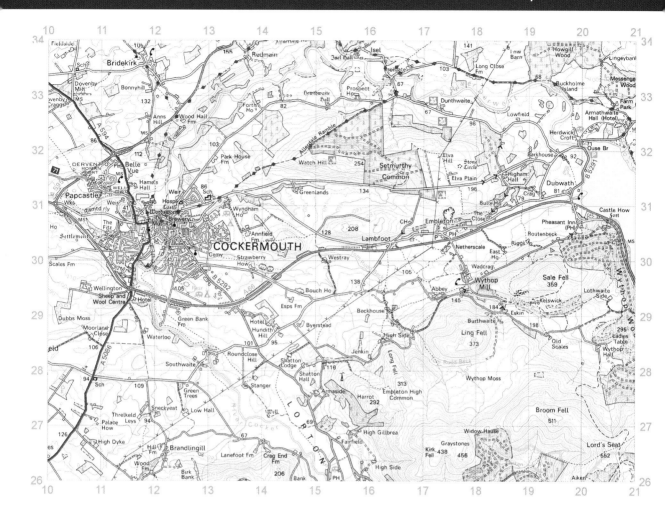

OS map extract of Cockermouth (not to scale)

Level 2

Exercise 3F

1. How could you recognise which weather system was affecting Britain by looking at the isobars on a weather map?

2. Describe the weather you would receive if the following weather systems were affecting Britain at the following times of year:
   (a) an anticyclone in February
   (b) a depression in March
   (c) an anticyclone in August

3. Why do most areas in Britain receive little convectional rainfall whereas places located along the Equator receive convectional rainfall on a daily basis?

3.4 A climate for concern and weather worries – syllabus extra/scholarship

What is being done to reduce the speed of climate change?

To reduce **global warming**, mankind needs to work together to reduce the amount of carbon dioxide being pumped into the atmosphere. One way to do this is to develop **renewable energy** resources to provide electricity instead of relying on burning **fossil fuels** like coal in power stations. Renewable energy resources include hydro electric power (HEP), solar, geothermal, tidal, wave and wind power. Another option is to develop nuclear power stations. On a local scale, individuals can help reduce global warming by saving energy in their homes and sharing car journeys.

Like most of the major oil companies, BP (British Petroleum) is now spending millions of pounds investing in new **bio fuels** that use a combination of traditional oil and oils derived from crops to power cars. Car manufacturers are aware that oil and therefore petrol supplies will run out shortly and that their customers are becoming increasingly concerned about the effect cars are having on the environment. Therefore all the major car manufacturers are developing car engines that can run on bio fuels and also batteries.

Extra example: Hurricane Frances, Florida 2004

Cause of the hurricane

Hurricanes are powerful tropical storms that generate winds of up to 200 km (125 miles) per hour and, when they move over land, can cause extensive damage to property and seriously threaten the lives of local residents. Hurricanes need specific conditions to develop so only occur in certain areas of the world. They are particularly common and destructive in the Gulf of Mexico affecting the islands of the Caribbean and southern states of the USA.

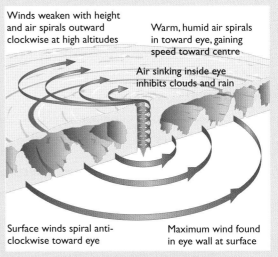

Fig. 3.4.1: Hurricane formation

Hurricanes start as a collection of storms over large areas of ocean that are very warm, crucially over 27°C. The very warm air from the storm and the ocean surface begins to rise. This creates low pressure at sea level. Winds blowing in the opposite direction cause the storm to start spinning and the rising warm air causes pressure to decrease at high altitudes. This draws in more and more warm air from the sea and sends cooler, drier air downwards. Heavy rain clouds form and thunderstorms develop. It becomes a hurricane when wind speeds reach 119 km (74 miles) per hour. The winds spiral around the area of very low pressure at the centre of the hurricane called the **eye**. Conditions on the ground below the eye are always calm as cool air gently sinks from the top of the hurricane down the eye. Moving away from the eye, however, wind speeds in the hurricane dramatically increase as air rushes into the hurricane at its base (see Fig. 3.4.1 on page 92).

Nature of Hurricane Frances

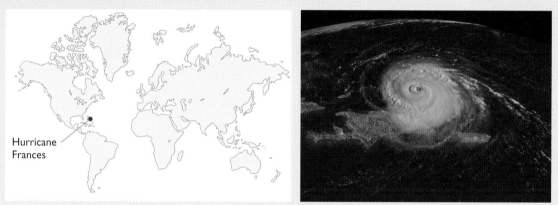

Fig. 3.4.2: Hurricane Frances – location and satellite image

In the late August of 2004, after the Gulf of Mexico had already experienced four hurricanes during the summer, a tropical storm began to develop in the north-west Atlantic Ocean. As it moved in a westerly direction and gained strength it was soon upgraded and given the name of Hurricane Frances.

Category 4 hurricane (SSHS – Saffir-Simpson Hurricane Scale)

Formed 25th August 2004

Lowest pressure 935 mbar (hPa) as the eye passes over Florida (5th September) and a cold, fine mist settles in a silent, eerie atmosphere. From 4th September dew forms on objects due to large amounts of water in the atmosphere.

Highest winds 145 mph (230 km/h) (1 minute sustained)

Dissipated 10th September 2004

Areas affected: British Virgin Islands, Puerto Rico, US Virgin Islands, Turks and Caicos Islands, Bahamas, Florida, Georgia, North and South Carolina, Ohio and other eastern states; and south-eastern Canada as a tropical depression that caused much flooding.

Effects of Hurricane Frances

Environmental

- Most of the storm's force was felt along the east coast with over 15 cm (6 in) of rain in a 24-hour period causing widespread flooding.

- Wind speeds reached in excess of 230 km (143 miles) per hour causing damage to trees and vegetation and affecting the habitats of animals.

- Fresh flood water flowed into the sea, changing the sea water and killing fish and other marine life.

Social

- From 3rd September 2.8 million people tried to evacuate the area and found many airlines already closed down.

- Driving safely was difficult due to slippery roads and 80 km (50 mph) gusts. Roads became jammed with traffic (4th September).

- The Florida citrus crop was extensively damaged.

- Damage to property was widespread with mounds of fallen ceiling tiles, insulation, ruined furniture, trees, debris littering the streets (8th September).

- Most of Florida's power went down due to line losses at and around the St Lucie Nuclear Power Plant. Power was 60% restored by 13th September.

- Total fatalities attributed to the hurricane were seven direct, 42 indirect.

Economic

- It is estimated that destruction to property caused by Hurricane Frances on the islands of the Bahamas cost around $600 million.

- The hurricane caused approximately $100 million damage to NASA space and military equipment at Cape Canaveral and ultimately cost the USA $9 billion, the fourth costliest hurricane ever.

- Total damages cost almost $10 billion.

Human response to the hurricane

- In the preparations for the hurricane the Governor of Florida declared a state of emergency.

- Many institutions such as schools, colleges and public buildings were closed (2nd September) and remained closed for some time.

- Following the disaster the President made Florida a federal disaster zone.

- The Red Cross provided warm meals twice a day for a week as well as water and other needs. The National Guard provided MREs (army field ration meals), water, ice and occasionally sheets of tarpaulin (6th September).

Fig. 3.4.3: Hurricane Frances battering Florida

See also *Geography ISEB Revision Guide* case study on hurricanes.

Exam tip

In the exam you are likely to be asked to discuss the formation or human impact of a weather hazard you have studied. When discussing the formation or cause of hurricanes it would be useful to draw a simple, well-labelled diagram to support your answer (see, for example, Fig. 3.4.1 page 92). If you are discussing the human impact of a hurricane make sure you say which hurricane example you are using and when it happened, and include as many facts as you can about the damage to property and risk to life that the hurricane caused.

Summary

Although gradual climate change is a natural process, human beings are causing the Earth's atmosphere to heat up at an increased rate by polluting it with carbon dioxide. A layer of carbon dioxide is trapping heat, causing global warming, which in turn is leading to problems such as coastal flooding. To reduce global warming we need to consider using renewable energy resources and nuclear power to generate power and find alternative fuels for our vehicles. The number of hurricanes experienced in the Gulf of Mexico is increasing due to higher ocean temperatures. One example is Hurricane Frances which caused extensive flooding, destruction to property and death in the Bahamas and Florida during August and September 2004.

Exercise 3G

1. (a) Describe what is meant by **global warming**.

   (b) What can governments and individuals do to slow down the rate of global warming?

2. Hurricanes only occur in specific areas of the world. Why is this?

3. Using the information in the text (pages 92–95), create a timeline of events to describe what happened as Hurricane Frances moved from the north-east Atlantic Ocean in a westerly direction over the Bahamas then Florida.

4. Imagine you were trapped in your hotel when Hurricane Frances passed over Florida. Write an account of what you would experience as the hurricane passed over. Do not forget that conditions are very different when the eye of the hurricane passes over.

Exercise 3H

1. Who should take the lead in trying to reduce carbon dioxide emissions into the atmosphere: the UN and EU, our government, multi-national companies or individuals?

2. Explain what precautions and procedures individuals should take to limit the damage and risk to life hurricanes can cause.

3. The east coast of Florida has always been a hazardous place to live during the late summer. Why has the hazard increased in recent years?

Exercise 3I: Enquiry suggestion

To analyse microclimate variations within your school or home grounds, you will need a set of outdoor thermometers to measure temperature variations and a set of rain gauges to measure precipitation variations. Choose at least four different sites around your school or home grounds that are different in their aspect and proximity to features that influence microclimate such as trees and buildings. Place a rain gauge and thermometer together at each site along with a note to explain that the equipment is being used for a microclimate experiment and should not be moved. Each day of the week at the same time record the temperature on the thermometer and measure the precipitation received in the rain gauge at each site. Do not forget to empty the rain gauge each time after measuring its contents. At the end of the week you will have enough data to analyse whether the aspect of and surrounding features at each site are influencing the microclimate.

Exercise 3J: Past exam questions

1. (a) What is a microclimate? (1 mark)

   (b) Name three factors which affect microclimates. (3 marks)

2. Look at the diagrammatic cross-section of the British Isles and answer the questions below.

   (a) Which letter best fits the area which is:

   (i) the warmest in winter

   (ii) the coldest all the year

   (iii) the wettest

   (iv) the driest? (4 marks)

   (b) Give a reason for your choice of the warmest location. (2 marks)

   (c) Give a reason for your choice of the wettest location. (2 marks)

3. Look at the map below and the annotations on the map. Explain the reasons why this pattern of rainfall occurs. (6 marks)

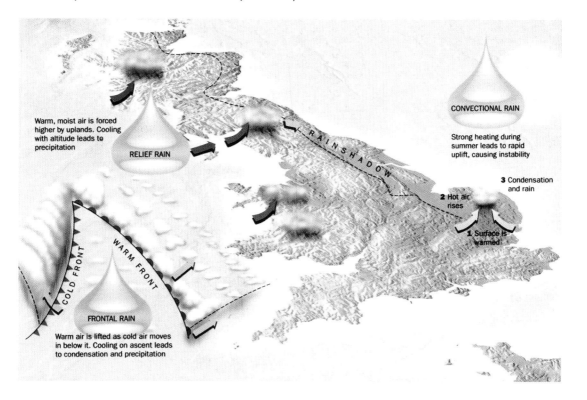

4. Study the three northern hemisphere climate graphs below and answer the questions which follow:

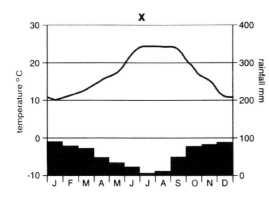

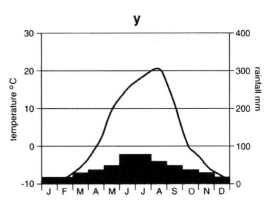

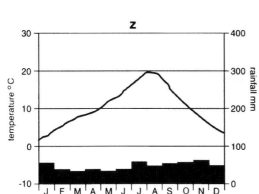

State which climate graph (**x, y** or **z**) has:
(i)   winter frosts
(ii) summer droughts
(iii) the smallest annual range of temperature
(iv) the smallest variation of precipitation throughout the year
(v)   the best climate for a warm, sunny and dry summer holiday. (4 marks)

5. Which of the following options (**i, ii** or **iii**) forms a correct statement?

(a) Condensation is
   (i)   water dropping from the clouds
   (ii) water vapour changing into tiny water droplets
   (iii) water changing into water vapour.

(b) The process by which water soaks into the ground is called
   (i) interception
   (ii) groundwater
   (iii) infiltration.

(c) Relief rainfall occurs when
   (i) two air masses meet
   (ii) there is a hill in the path of a warm air mass
   (iii) the land and water is heated by the sun.

(d) The British Isles enjoys a temperate climate. This means that
   (i) sunshine rates are very high throughout the year
   (ii) rainfall and temperature are similar throughout the year
   (iii) it is never very hot or cold, and is rarely very wet or dry. (4 marks)

Exercise 3K: Scholarship or more advanced question

Weather maps in newspapers and on television often look very simple, but the weather they describe can be very difficult to understand fully. Why is this? (25 marks)

Exercise 3L

Solve the following clues.

1. Person who studies the weather (13 letters)
2. The distance of a place north or south of the Equator (8 letters)
3. Man-made structures that influence microclimate (9 letters)
4. The moisture content of the air (8 letters)
5. The climate of a specific and small area (12 letters)
6. Word describing Britain's weather (4 letters)
7. Line linking areas of equal temperature on a weather chart (8 letters)
8. Scale used to measure strength of the wind (8 letters)
9. A large body of air with similar moisture and temperature characteristics (3 letters + 4 letters)
10. A change in the state of water in the water cycle (8 letters)

Weather and climate glossary

Air mass	A large body of air with consistent moisture and temperature characteristics.
Air pressure	The weight of the air measured in millibars.
Altitude	The height of a place measured in metres above sea level.
Anemometer	Instrument used to measure wind speed.
Anticyclone	A high pressure weather system associated with still and cold weather in winter and still and warm weather in summer.
Aspect	The direction a slope faces in relation to the Sun.
Atmosphere	The air surrounding the Earth.
Barometer	Instrument used to measure air pressure.
Beaufort scale	A scale measuring wind speed.
Bio fuels	Fuels made from products derived from crops sometimes combined with traditional petroleum based fuels.
Climate	The temperature and rainfall of a region measured over a number of years.
Condensation	Water droplets that are produced when water vapour is cooled and forms clouds.
Convectional rainfall	Rain that is produced when air rises as the ground is heated by the Sun.
Depression	A low pressure weather system associated with wet and windy weather throughout the year.
Equatorial climate	A climate band stretching either side of the Equator which is wet and hot throughout the year.
Evaporation	When water is turned from a liquid into a gas (water vapour) due to heating by the Sun.
Eye	Centre of hurricane where winds are light.
Fossil fuels	Non-renewable resources that pollute the atmosphere with carbon dioxide, e.g. coal, oil and natural gas.
Front	The divide between warm and cold air masses; associated with rainfall.

Frontal rainfall	Rain that is produced when warm air is forced to rise over cold air at a front.
Global warming	Rapid heating of the Earth's atmosphere caused by the build-up of carbon dioxide.
Groundwater	Water held in or moving through permeable rock.
Gulf Stream	A current of warm water that flows from the Gulf of Mexico to the south-west of Britain in winter. See North Atlantic Drift.
Humidity	The moisture content of the air.
Hydrological cycle	The constant interchange of water between the sea, the land and the air. See Water cycle.
Interception	When precipitation lands and is absorbed by vegetation and buildings.
Isobar	A line on a map joining places of the same air pressure.
Isotherm	A line on a map joining places of the same temperature.
Latitude	The distance of a place north or south of the Equator.
Meteorologists	Scientists who study the weather.
Microclimate	The climate of a specific and small area (e.g. your school grounds).
Monsoon	Winds that bring prolonged periods of heavy rainfall to a large region of south east Asia.
North Atlantic Drift	The warm flow of water that comes from the Gulf of Mexico and warms the west coast of Britain in winter. See Gulf Stream.
Peninsula	Land protruding into the sea.
Permeable rock	Rock that allows water to be held within it or flow through it.
Precipitation	Water droplets falling to the ground once the clouds have cooled to a point where they can no longer hold their moisture. Precipitation can take the form of rain, snow, sleet and hail.
Prevailing wind	A wind from the predominant, or most usual, direction. The prevailing wind in Britain is from the south-west.

Rain gauge	Instrument used to measure precipitation.
Rainshadow	Area on the eastern side of mountain ranges in Britain which receives less rainfall due to protection afforded by the mountains from the south-westerly prevailing winds.
Relief	Geographical term that describes the height of the land.
Relief rainfall	Rain caused by air being forced to rise rapidly over hills and mountains leading to rapid condensation and precipitation.
Renewable energy	Energy created with resources that will not run out and which do not pollute the atmosphere, e.g. solar, wind, HEP.
Stevenson screen	Weather station housing instruments such as a barometer and maximum/minimum thermometer.
Temperate maritime	Term used to describe climates that are similar to Britain's; warm summers and mild winters with rainfall occurring throughout the year.
Temperature range	Difference between maximum and minimum temperature over a 24-hour period.
Throughflow	The flow of groundwater through saturated soils.
Transfers	Movements of water within the water cycle from one area of storage or state to another. For example, water changing from liquid to water vapour as it is evaporated.
Transpiration	When water from plants and trees is evaporated from their leaves.
Water cycle	The constant interchange of water between the sea, the land and the air. See Hydrological cycle.
Water vapour	Evaporated water held as a gas within the atmosphere.
Weather	The atmospheric conditions (temperature, rainfall, air pressure, wind speed and direction) of a region measured over a short period of time.

Chapter 4: Settlement

Syllabus extra

Note that the ISEB syllabus only requires you to cover certain elements of settlements and this section gives an extended background to the type of questions on settlement that may arise in the mapwork section of the CE exam.

A typical London street scene

A settlement is a place where people live. These places vary in size from tiny hamlets, where there may only be a few houses and no services, to megacities where the population may exceed 10 million people. This chapter will look at:

● Why people first decided to live in a fixed place.

● What factors they had to consider when choosing a place for a settlement.

● How the shape of settlements change over time.

● The causes and effects of different types of migration.

A British town scene

A view of a UK village

4.1 The site and situation of a settlement

A background to settlements in Britain

There was a time when Britain was populated by tribes that may have occupied a region but did not live permanently in one place. Instead, these tribes moved around the region hunting and gathering food. A mobile population such as this is known as **nomadic**, and such communities still exist in many parts of the world.

However, approximately 10 000 years ago these nomadic populations developed the ability to grow crops from seed, rather than just gather edible wild vegetation, and rear animals for their young. Thus farming, or **agriculture** as we know it today, began. Growing crops from seed and rearing animals in enclosures required these previously nomadic populations to stay in one place, and therefore the first settlements were developed.

Soon after people settled in one place they began to trade. Most farmers grew crops and reared animals for consumption by their own family. This method of farming is called **subsistence farming**. However, during a good season a farmer may produce too many crops; this extra produce is called a **surplus**. Rather than let it go to waste a farmer would rather sell his surplus within his **settlement**, or more likely, to people from other settlements who had not produced as much. This, in turn, led to trade between settlements and the development of early transport routes between settlements, many of which form the basis of roads we use today.

When we begin to think about the reasons why a certain place was chosen for a settlement it is important to remember that many settlements are very old. This is especially true in Britain, as many of our settlements were first built hundreds if not thousands of years ago. For example, the two OS map extracts in this chapter (pages 132 and 133) are of Sheffield which is believed to have been first settled in the 12th century, although there are many older examples than this in Britain.

Site factors

When early settlers were choosing a suitable place to build a settlement, they would have considered various factors. These **site factors** (see Fig. 4.1.1 page 105), were likely to be related to the **physical landscape** of the area.

Water supply

Unlike today, water was not readily available from a tap and a fresh water supply was vital for a settlement to exist. Rivers were generally less polluted than they are today and were an obvious supply of fresh water, as were springs and wells.

Defence

Settling populations needed to consider defending themselves against other rival tribes in the region and later against invading armies from Europe. A site on the inside of a river meander or near or on a hill-top is easier to defend than other locations.

Bridging points / fords

Settlers were likely to cross a river at a shallow point and then build a bridge in this position. Once established, a bridge would act as a trading route for settlements situated either side of the river.

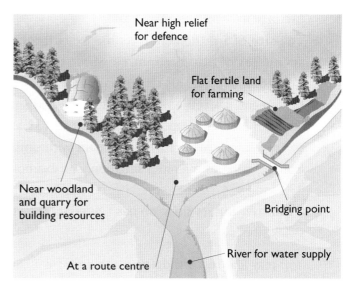

Fig. 4.1.1: A sketch illustrating the six site factors

Route centres and transport

Certain locations have been natural route meeting points for thousands of years due to their physical landscape. For example, the routes used by locals and traders at the bottom of valleys meet where two or more valleys converge. These ancient routes may have developed into modern roads and the route centres into large settlements.

Farming

A site that offered flat land either side of a river (**floodplain**) would be attractive to early settlers as farming was a necessity to feed people. Being too close to the river would bring the danger of flooding, however, so settlements were often located higher up the floodplain. Due to the growth of settlements most modern settlements have now built on their floodplains.

Building materials and fuel

Early societies needed easily accessible resources close by. Proximity to woodland was useful as timber could be used for several purposes including house building, boat construction and as a fuel for cooking and heating. Easily quarried stone was also a valuable resource for building.

Situation

The **site** of a settlement is its the exact location (originally resulting from various advantages of that location). However, the physical geography of the land surrounding the settlement was also important to early settlers and this is called the **situation** of a settlement. If a settlement had several good site factors and a good situation, such as Sheffield (see OS map on pages 132 and 133 and Fig. 4.1.2 below) it had the potential to grow into a large city. A settlement with similarly good site factors may be prevented from growing by a limited situation. For example, Oughtibridge (see OS map on page 132 and Fig. 4.1.3) has several good site factors such as a bridging point, a route centre and a river but its situation has limited its growth as it is surrounded by steep-sided valley slopes.

You may like to consider the site and the situation of your school.

The site and situation of Sheffield

Sheffield has grown into a large city with a population recorded at the 2001 census of 513 234. Like all settlements, it started with just a few houses and a very small population, but Sheffield has grown due to some of the following site and situation factors. Use the OS map on page 133 to identify each one.

(1) It has a water supply in the River Don (grid square (GS): 3291).

(2) It has high ground which would have been useful for defence (GS: 3489).

(3) It has a series of bridging points (GS: 3588).

(4) It is a natural route centre located at the head of three valleys – the River Don, River Loxley and River Riveline (GS: 3289/3489).

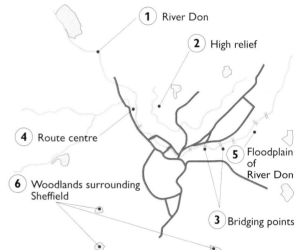

Fig. 4.1.2: An annotated sketch map showing Sheffield's site factors and situation

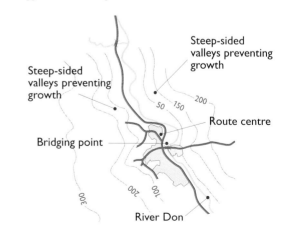

Fig. 4.1.3: An annotated sketch map showing Oughtibridge's site factors and situation

(5) The floodplain of the River Don would have provided excellent farmland, although it has now been developed (GS: 3888).

(6) There are woodlands surrounding Sheffield (GS: 3294).

It is not always possible fully to identify reasons for a settlement's growth from a map. Sheffield grew initially due to the wool trade in the 13th century, using wool from sheep grazing on the Pennines. Later, with the advent of the **Industrial Revolution** in the late 18th and early 19th century, Sheffield's population increased rapidly when people from surrounding **rural** areas came to live in Sheffield and work in the iron and steel factories.

Exam tip
When answering an exam question about the original site factors of a settlement, think about what would have happened in the past. You are likely to be asked to quote evidence from an OS map to support your answer; look for castles, rivers, cathedrals, bridging points and route centres.

Summary
People began to live in settlements when they learnt how to farm and therefore needed to stay in one place. Places chosen as settlements had a physical landscape with good site factors, the most important original site factor being water supply. The situation of a settlement is its location in relation to the surrounding physical landscape. If the situation had resources such as wood, stone and coal, this would have helped the settlement to grow.

Exercise 4A

1. Explain why people decided to live in a fixed place in Britain 10 000 years ago.

2. What does the term 'surplus' mean?

3. For what reasons do you think Sheffield grew into the city of over half a million people that it is today?

4. Why has Oughtibridge not grown in the same way that Sheffield has?

5. Look at the OS maps in this book of settlements other than Sheffield (pages 28–31, 65, 91). Try to identify the original site factors for another settlement.

Exercise 4B

1. Why did agriculture replace a nomadic life for those living in Britain 10 000 years ago?

2. Explain how agricultural surpluses led to trade between settlements.

3. Explain why some settlements grow steadily over the centuries whereas others show very little population change. Refer to examples in your answer.

4. Settlements may appear to be randomly scattered on our landscape. Is this the case?

4.2 Settlement patterns and functions

Settlement patterns

There are three principal **settlement pattern**s or shapes (see Fig. 4.2.1 pages 109–110):

- **linear settlements**, where the buildings are arranged in a line

- **nucleated settlements**, where the buildings are arranged around a central point

- **dispersed settlements**, where the buildings are few in number and well away from other settlements.

It is very difficult to know what pattern a settlement is when you are actually in, or driving through, that settlement. However, if you see the settlement from above, the bird's eye or **plan view**, it becomes a lot clearer. You might have seen settlement patterns from above when looking out of the window of an aeroplane, but the easiest way to see the pattern of a settlement is by looking at a map.

Many settlements in Britain fit into these three categories of settlement pattern and there are few new settlements being built; it is much more likely that older settlements will expand. However, there is another category called **planned settlements**, where new settlements are built from scratch and in a well planned, ordered fashion. Such new planned settlements are more likely to be found in LEDC countries (e.g. Brasilia in Brazil).

Reasons for settlement patterns

Just as there is always a reason why a settlement is first settled, there is always a good reason why it grows in the pattern it does.

Nucleated comes from the word 'nucleus' meaning a core or central point. Nucleated settlements can grow around a number of different features at their core. Very commonly this may be a crossroads where people have decided to settle and trade. Smaller nucleated villages may have a village green at their core, which would have served as a market place in years gone by but is most likely to be used for recreation today. Nucleated settlements could also be built around such features as a river confluence, a bridging point or ford, a castle, a cathedral or a market place.

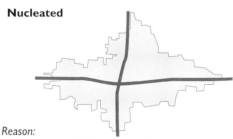

Nucleated

Reason:
- Crossroads • Market place • Castle at centre
- Bridging point/ford • Village green
- River confluence • Cathedral at centre

Fig. 4.2.1a A nucleated settlement – Bisley, Gloucestershire

Linear

Reason:
- Road between two larger settlements • River
- Valley bottom • Coast/large lake frontage

Fig. 4.2.1b A linear settlement – Brooksby, Leicestershire

Linear comes from the word 'line'. A linear settlement, or **ribbon settlement**, is arranged in a line, though this does not have to be a straight line. The most common place to find linear settlements is along a main road leading to a large settlement or on a main road between two larger settlements. Linear settlements may also be found tracing the course of a river along the bottom of a valley. The presence of the sea means that along coastlines, settlements sometimes spread out in a linear fashion. Along the shores of large lakes, settlements grow in a linear fashion to make the most of waterside frontage (e.g. Lake Leman, Switzerland).

Dispersed

Reason:
• Farmland • High relief
• Physical landscape (forest/lakes/desert)

Fig. 4.2.1c A dispersed settlement – Little Haresfield, Gloucestershire

Dispersed means 'spread out'. Dispersed settlements are located in rural areas away from other settlements. They may be made up of just a few houses or may be of hamlet size, but there is always a reason for their distance from other settlements. In Britain this is usually because the land is needed for farming so cannot be built on. However, it is often the physical landscape that limits the growth of settlements and this causes the settlement pattern to be dispersed. Dense forest causes settlements to be dispersed in tropical areas such as Brazil, high **relief** is the cause in mountainous countries such as Nepal, a high density of lakes is the cause in countries like Finland, and a barren desert landscape causes settlements to be dispersed in regions such as the Sahara in western Africa.

Fig. 4.2.2: A centre for commerce and leisure

Settlement functions

The **functions** of a settlement are the reasons why it has grown and the purpose of the settlement: the things that happen there. The functions of settlements may be split into six groups. A settlement may begin with just one function and then over time develop more functions. The functions of a settlement may change as well as grow.

Commercial

Most settlements have some form of commercial function. This means they have shopping facilities ranging from a small shop in a village to shopping malls in towns and cities. Commercial functions can also include facilities such as cinemas and sports centres.

Residential

All settlements have a residential function. However, some settlements are built purposely to provide homes for people, often outside a city due to overcrowding in the centre. **Dormitory settlements** are settlements that are close to larger settlements and where many of the inhabitants **commute** into the city to work each day.

Administrative

Larger settlements often have an administrative function. This means that local government has central offices in the settlement from which it runs public services such as waste disposal and library services.

Industrial

Settlements of all different sizes may have an industrial function. This means that companies that make (manufacture) something locate their factory in the settlement. Big cities tend to have many industries because these industries need a lot of people to work in their factories. However, some industries may wish to locate near smaller settlements because the land price may be cheaper.

Tourism

Different kinds of settlement may have a tourist function due to different reasons. Big cities have the attraction of museums, art galleries and major sports facilities. Small villages in beautiful countryside have the attraction of outside sports and the quiet rural life.

Services

As the size of a settlement increases, the range and number of **services** increase. Services include things such as doctors' surgeries, hospitals and schools. A small village may have none of these services, whereas a major city will have many.

Exam tip

When identifying the pattern of a settlement on an OS map, try to identify the cause of the settlement growing in this pattern because if you can find the cause you are probably right about which pattern it is.

If you are asked to identify the functions of a settlement from an OS map, even if it is in an extremely rural area, the settlement will have a residential function as all settlements have this function.

Summary

There are three settlement patterns you need to be able to recognise on an OS map:

- Linear settlements are found in a line, often along a main road.

- Nucleated settlements are grouped around a central point, commonly a crossroads.

- Dispersed settlements are small and spread out, often because the relief is high.

The function of a settlement is its purpose. A settlement's functions may change over time. Settlements that continue to grow increase the number of functions that they offer their residents.

Exercise 4C

1. Draw simple diagrams to show the three settlement patterns.

2. For each settlement pattern describe what could cause the settlement to have grown like this.

3. What is meant by the term 'settlement function'?

4. What are the functions of your local town or city? What evidence do you have to support your answer?

5. Use the OS map extract of Sheffield (pages 132 and 133) to find evidence of Sheffield's functions. Give a four figure grid reference for each piece of evidence.

6. Name two places in the world that have mostly dispersed settlements. Explain your choices.

Level 2

Exercise 4D

1. Look at the OS map extract of Sheffield (pages 132 and 133). Find a linear settlement and draw a sketch of it including details such as buildings, roads, rivers and contour lines. Give your sketch a clear title.

2. Give the six figure grid reference of any dispersed settlements on the map. Identify why you think they are dispersed. Quote map evidence in your answer.

3. Why are nucleated settlements the most common type of settlement? Illustrate your answer with examples.

4.3 The settlement hierarchy, shops and services

Settlements in a hierarchy

The word **hierarchy** describes putting things in order, giving something a rank or priority. It can be applied to different subjects. For example, you rank football teams by which division they are in and, within their divisions, by how many points they have. The football hierarchy is seen as tables but hierarchies are more commonly represented as pyramids (see Fig. 4.3.1). Using a pyramid with bands to split it, it should be possible for you to create a hierarchy of people within your school with the headteacher at the top.

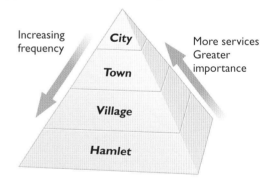

Broadly, we split the settlement hierarchy up into four, with cities in the top band of the hierarchy, followed by towns, villages and then hamlets. As the pyramid indicates, the further you go up the settlement hierarchy the more important the settlement will be, as it will have more services and functions. As you go

Fig. 4.3.1: The settlement hierarchy

down the hierarchy the frequency or number of settlements increases. So there will be more hamlets than villages, more villages than towns and so on.

City, town, village or hamlet?

Deciding whether a settlement is a city, town, village or hamlet is not as simple as you may think, and those in power within local and central government both influence this process of categorising settlements. Three factors are taken into consideration:

● the number of services the settlement offers and how far people will come to use these services (the **range**).

- the population size of the settlement

- the distance the settlement is from other settlements. Therefore, large settlements such as cities will be far apart from each other, whereas smaller settlements such as hamlets could be very close to other hamlets.

These three factors are summarised below:

Fig. 4.3.2: Categorising settlements

	Cities	Towns	Villages	Hamlets
Typical services	MANY			FEW
	Many schools Shopping complex University Cathedral Hospitals Sports stadiums Many hotels Department stores	Railway station Town hall Cinema Shopping arcade Secondary schools Bus station Banks	Doctor's surgery Primary school Public house Village hall	None
Typical population	HIGH			LOW
	Over 100 000	1000 to 100 000	20 to 1000	Under 20
Typical distance apart	FAR			NEAR
	Up to 160 km (100 miles)	40–80 km (25–50 miles)	8–16 km (5–10 miles)	1.5–3 km (1–2 miles)

Look at the OS map extracts of Sheffield on pages 132 and 133. The settlement hierarchy is evident on this map. There is one city (Sheffield) which is surrounded by several villages (Thorpe Hesley 3796, Dungworth 2889, etc.) and many hamlets (Storrs 2989, Hollow Meadows 2488, etc) in the rural area beyond the city limits. Chapeltown 3596 is not a town but is in fact a **suburb** of the city of Sheffield. There are no towns on the OS map extract of Sheffield. Why do you think this is?

Shops and services

Have you ever thought about what type of shops and services you get in different types of settlement? You may have noticed that in villages you often only find a newsagent and a primary school whereas large towns or cities have big department stores, restaurants, hotels, cinemas and many more different shops and services.

A summary of the shops and services offered by a typical settlement at each band of the settlement hierarchy is shown in Fig. 4.3.2 on page 114.

A minimum population level is necessary for a settlement to support different shops and services. This minimum population number is called the **threshold**. For example, to have a village shop it is estimated that a village must have at least 300 people living in it (a threshold of 300 people). The threshold for a large department store such as Debenhams is much higher, demanding a minimum population of nearer 100 000 people. Therefore we only see department stores in cities.

A local convenience shop

A large department store

Fig. 4.3.3: Outlets for convenience goods and comparison goods

The range of a shop is the distance people are prepared to travel to reach it and the **catchment area** is where those people are living. The range depends on the type of goods the shop is selling. A village shop sells goods that we buy on a daily basis such as bread, milk and newspapers. We call these **convenience goods** and would not be prepared to travel very far to buy them. A village shop selling convenience goods would therefore have a small range and would be called a **low order service**. An electrical shop sells much more expensive items such as personal computers and DVD players. Customers will compare the price of these items at other electrical shops before buying. We call these **comparison goods**, and customers would travel into the city to buy them. A shop selling comparison goods, said to be a **high order service**, would therefore have a large range.

Public services such as libraries, schools and hospitals also have a threshold and range. You might expect to find a primary school in a village as it will have a low threshold and small range. However, you would expect to find a large hospital in a city because it has a high threshold and large range. For example, Sheffield has a large hospital. Look at the OS map extract on page 133, grid square 3690.

Out of town shopping centres

We all know that if you want to go shopping in most settlements you head for the town or city centre, which we call the **Central Business District** (**CBD**). But not all shops are found in the middle of the city; in fact since 1980 there has been a steady increase in the number of out of town shopping centres being built in or beyond the outer suburbs of Britain's cities.

Out of town shopping centres are large developments of shops, restaurants and entertainment facilities that are built on sites away from the city because of the specific advantages of these locations, some of which are listed below.

- Close to a motorway junction providing good access to a large catchment area.

- Close to an **arterial road** linking the out of town shopping centre with the CBD and other areas of the nearest city, or a **bypass** making it accessible to the surrounding area.

- Built on cheaper land as it is away from the centre of the city.

- Built on a site with lots of space available for parking.

Out of town shopping centres have a large range and attract customers from urban areas across a large region. However, they are normally located in, or just beyond, the outer suburbs of one particular city, and therefore might take business away from shops located in the CBD of that city. There may be some positive effects of fewer people visiting the CBD such as less traffic congestion and less pollution, but negative effects include unemployment in the CBD and vandalism of shops that have been boarded up after closing down.

On the OS map extract of Sheffield on page 133 you can see Meadowhall shopping centre at grid reference 393900. Meadowhall was built on this site in 1990 and boasts over 270 different shops, its own cinema and a food court. It has excellent transport links with the rest of Sheffield, having its own train and tram stations, as well as being located on one of the main bus and car routes into the centre of Sheffield. The nearby motorway junction of the M1 means that Meadowhall is within one hour's drive of nine other cities including Rotherham, Doncaster and Barnsley. You can find out more about Meadowhall by looking at its website (www.meadowhall.co.uk).

Since Meadowhall opened in 1990 it has been reported that takings at shops in Sheffield's CBD have been reduced by 25% and many have been forced to close down. Empty shops have been targeted by graffiti and therefore make the city centre less attractive, which in turn deters new businesses from starting up in the CBD.

Summary

Settlements are often seen in a hierarchy. This means they are organised in order of their importance with cities at the top of the hierarchy and hamlets at the bottom of the hierarchy. The position of a settlement within the hierarchy depends on the number of services it has, its population and its distance from other similar settlements.

Smaller settlements have shops selling convenience goods because they have a low threshold and small range. Larger settlements will have shops selling comparison goods because they have a high threshold and large range. These settlements may have out of town shopping centres in their suburbs which may take business away from shops in the CBD.

Exercise 4E

Level 1

1. Make a simple copy of Fig. 4.3.1 (page 113). Add to it an example of a hamlet, village, town and city from your local area.

2. Look at the OS map extract of Sheffield on page 132. In grid square 3092 you will see a settlement called Worrall. What type of settlement is this: a hamlet, village, town or city? Give reasons for your answer referring to map evidence.

3. OS maps do not show individual shops so we cannot tell what shops there are in Worrall. Would you expect to find convenience or comparison goods for sale in a shop in Worrall? Give a reason for your answer using the terms 'threshold' and 'range'.

4. Draw a spider diagram to show the advantages of the site that was chosen for the location of Meadowhall shopping centre (see the OS map extract of Sheffield on page 133, grid reference 393909).

5. What problems can the building of out of town shopping centres in the city suburbs have on the CBD of the city?

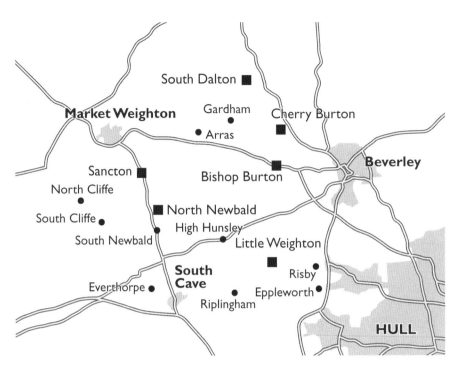

Fig. 4.3.4: Settlements in South Yorkshire

Exercise 4F

1. Rearrange the settlements in the South Yorkshire extract above into a triangular settlement hierarchy as in Fig. 4.3.1 (page 113).

2. Look at the OS map extract of Sheffield on pages 132 and 133. If Debenhams were going to build a new department store in this area, in which of the following grid squares do you think it would be put: 3092, 3990 or 3587? Discuss the advantages and disadvantages of each site using some of the following terms: hierarchy; range or catchment area; threshold; convenience goods or low order services; comparison goods or high order services; Central Business District.

3. Use the OS map extract of Sheffield on page 133 to identify specific map evidence that shows why Meadowhall shopping centre was built where it was. Can you identify any other sites on the OS map extract of Sheffield (pages 132 and 133) that might have been suitable for an out of town shopping centre? Give reasons for your choices.

4. Draw a flow chart to illustrate the problems that can be caused for businesses and the environment in the CBD when an out of town shopping centre opens in the suburbs of the city.

4.4 Urban land use patterns in Britain

Land use in urban areas

Land use is the way the land is utilised, whether it is for housing, offices, factories, entertainment facilities, colleges or universities, or simply left as open parkland. **Urban** areas, our towns and cities, have many different land uses which can change very quickly as you move from one part of a town or city to another. Think about your nearest urban area. Can you identify how the land use changes from one part of this town or city to another? Although all cities are different you may be surprised to learn that they often have very similar land uses which are often located in very similar parts of the city. Because of this, geographers have been able to create a general diagram, called a **model**, which shows what the different land uses in different parts of an average city might be. In this model, a simple and clear pattern emerges, showing changing land use in a circular pattern coming out from the city centre (the CBD).

The concentric circle model

You have already seen a geographical model in the form of a settlement hierarchy (see page 113). Models are simplified versions of reality, therefore no region will fit perfectly into the settlement hierarchy and no city will fit perfectly into the pattern the concentric circle model suggests. This model applies to cities in **MEDCs**; a different model needs to be drawn for the land use pattern in **LEDCs**. Here we see four parts of the city and how three patterns emerge as you travel from the outskirts of the city towards the CBD.

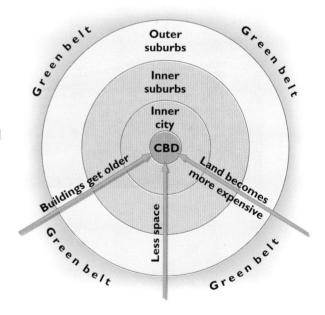

Fig. 4.4.1: The concentric circle model

- The age of buildings increases. The oldest buildings will be in the centre where the city began.

- Land becomes more expensive as more value is placed on property within easy reach of the facilities of the CBD.

- The amount of space decreases as housing becomes more compact nearer to the CBD, in order to allow as many people as possible to have a short commute to the CBD.

Land use in the concentric circle model

CBD	Inner city	Inner suburbs	Outer suburbs	Country-side
• Old buildings • Modernised buildings • Shops • Offices • Entertainment • Restaurants • Train/bus station • Flats	• Terraced housing • Flats • Converted factories • Modernised housing • Art galleries	• Semi-detached housing • Convenience goods shops • Schools	• Detached houses • Hospitals • Out of town shopping centres • Park land • Stadiums • Industrial estates • Ring road	• Farmland • Green belt

Fig. 4.4.2: Land use in each part of the concentric circle model

CBD – civic amenities

Inner city – terraced housing

Inner suburbs – semi-detached housing

Outer suburbs – a shopping centre

Fig. 4.4.3: Land use in Sheffield from each part of the concentric circle model

The simplest concentric circle model has four parts. Fig. 4.4.2 (page 120) shows what the land use might be in each of the four parts of the city. The very centre of the city is known as the Central Business District (CBD). This is likely to be where the city first started and you may be able to find map evidence for this, such as a bridging point or route centre. The CBD may contain old buildings as it was the likely starting point of the city but will also have modern buildings and old buildings that have been **modernised**. The CBD will have lots of shops, restaurants and entertainment facilities such as nightclubs and bars. It will also have office blocks but only a small amount of land in the CBD will be given to housing, which might be in apartment blocks due to the very limited space available. The CBD will be the meeting point for transport in the city so you will find train, bus and tram stations all located in the CBD.

Moving away from the CBD, the next zone in the concentric circle model is called the **inner city**. Typically you will find **terraced housing** in this zone. These houses are small, arranged in rows and old as they were built to accommodate factory workers during the Industrial Revolution. Factories have since relocated to the **outer suburbs** due to the cheaper land and space for expansion. Old factories, commonly mills, have therefore been converted into other land uses such as housing, museums or art galleries, a process known as **urban renewal**. The Tate Modern art gallery, located in London's inner city zone, was a former power station which closed in 1982.

The **inner suburbs** form the next zone of the city. The land in the inner suburbs is mostly given to housing. As there is more space in the inner suburbs the housing tends to be larger and **semi-detached**, and many of the houses have gardens and garages. As this zone of the city has been built more recently, housing also tends to be newer and is occasionally accompanied by schools and shops selling convenience goods.

The final outer zone of the city is called the outer suburbs. There are a variety of different land uses in this zone because there is a lot more space, the land is cheaper and ring roads give good access. Houses in the outer suburbs tend to be large and **detached** and have large gardens. The outer suburbs may also contain sports stadiums, hospitals, universities, council estates, industrial estates and out of town shopping centres.

Limiting urban growth

Strict laws are in place in most MEDCs to prevent cities growing out of control. If there were no such laws, cities would continually spread outwards, a process known as **urban sprawl** or **urbanisation**. When planning laws were less strict in Britain, urban sprawl led to cities that were once many miles apart growing together to form one large urban area called a **conurbation**. For example, in Britain, Manchester and

Liverpool have grown together, as have Leeds and Bradford. There are many planning laws set down by central and local government but the most well-known is the **green belt**. The green belt is an area surrounding a city within which you have to have very special permission to build new property, or even to change the shape or use of existing property.

Does Sheffield fit the concentric circle model?

Not all cities fit the patterns shown by the concentric circle model. Often physical features such as the coastline or steep hills direct the growth of a city into a different shape. For example, cities close to the sea will spread along the coastline in a linear fashion. Mountains might hamper the growth of an urban area in a certain direction. Folkestone in Kent is limited by steep relief in one direction and coastline in another.

Look at the OS map extract on pages 132 and 133. Do you think Sheffield fits the patterns shown in the concentric circle model? Certainly urban growth is limited to the west by high relief and the planning restrictions imposed by the national park (indicated by the yellow boundary). However, if you follow the A6135 from Sheffield's CBD to the outer suburbs you should find evidence that land use changes in a way that fits the concentric circle model.

Summary

What is built upon a piece of land is called the land use. Geographers are able to simplify the different land uses in a city by creating a model. A typical city has four broad zones of land use that are arranged in a concentric circle pattern:

- the CBD
- the inner city
- the inner suburbs
- the outer suburbs.

As you move from the outer suburbs towards the CBD the buildings get older, the price of land becomes more expensive and there is less space. Attempts have been made to stop the continual outward growth of cities (urban sprawl) by the creation of green belts around many urban areas.

Exercise 4G

1. Write at least two lines each to explain the meaning of the following terms, giving examples:
   (a) land use
   (b) geographical model

2. Make a larger copy of Fig. 4.4.1 (page 119), adding some of the detail of land use in each zone from Fig. 4.4.2 (page 120).

3. What patterns does the concentric circle model show about a typical city in an MEDC?

4. How does the type of housing change as you travel from the outer suburbs towards the CBD?

5. What is urban sprawl and what can be done to prevent it? Use examples in your answer.

Exercise 4H

1. Write half a page to discuss the changes in land use that emerge as you travel from the outer suburbs towards the CBD. Indicate patterns that are evident and give examples of land use.

2. Why do you think we get shopping facilities in the CBD, but also often in the outer suburbs in out of town shopping centres?

3. Giving map evidence from the extracts on pages 132 and 133, explain whether you think Sheffield does or does not fit into the patterns shown by the concentric circle model.

4. Do you think your local town or city fits the concentric circle model? Give reasons for your answer.

5. Conurbations are a result of urban sprawl. Discuss this statement and refer to examples of planning law.

4.5 The effects of migration on settlements – syllabus extra/scholarship

What is migration?

Migration is the term used to describe the movement of people from one place to another. There are several types of migration. We call the groups of people involved in these different types of migration different names. It is important not to confuse them.

International migration is when people move from one country to another. This may be a permanent move for the rest of their lives or simply a temporary move for a number of months or years. All people moving from one place to another are called migrants. The process of moving from one country to another is called **emigration** and people who have moved into a country from their own are called **immigrants**. Normally temporary migrants move to a different country because they are taking a job contract in that country. Such migrants have the choice to move so they are also referred to as voluntary migrants. You may have lived abroad with your parents because they decided to take a job in a different country for a period of time. Permanent migration is more likely to be the result of people seeking a better lifestyle or standard of living. The table below gives more reasons for temporary and permanent migration.

Fig. 4.5.1: Push and pull factors

Push factors	Pull factors
● War	● Better jobs
● Famine	● Attractive environment
● Natural disasters	● Better standard of living
● Unemployment	● Family members to join
● Drought	● Better education / health services

What causes migration?

The causes of any form of migration can be split into **push factors**, reasons why people want to leave a place, and **pull factors**, reasons why people are attracted to a different place. These are listed in Fig. 4.5.1 page 124. It is usually a combination of push and pull factors that causes voluntary migrants to migrate whether temporarily or permanently. A poor standard of living and lack of jobs are the most common push factors while the prospect of better paid jobs and a higher standard of services such as education and health are the most common pull factors. Sometimes a member of a family may have already emigrated to a different country and other family members follow.

Fig. 4.5.2: Refugees in Sudan as a result of famine

Unfortunately many migrants are forced to move either within a country or from one country to another due to problems where they live that are out of their control. These problems may include war, or natural disasters such as famine or floods. These forced migrants are referred to as **refugees**. People who enter another country for work or in search of a higher standard of living without permission are called **illegal immigrants**.

Migration in LEDCs

Often natural disasters such as famine and man-made problems such as war occur in LEDCs. Such events lead to forced migration with people leaving a region or country. Sometimes this may mean people are refugees in another country for a number of weeks or months but it may lead to permanent migration.

The most common process of migration in an LEDC, however, is the movement of people from the countryside to the city; this is called **rural-urban migration**. It is a constant process and occurs because those living in rural areas who are very poor and struggling to make a living from farming believe they will be able to find a

Fig. 4.5.3: A shanty town in Brazil

job and have a better standard of living in the city. Unfortunately, often migrants find there are no jobs available in the city and they are forced to make their own shelters to live in along with other migrants in what are called **shanty towns**.

Migration in Britain

In Britain, a large amount of rural-urban migration took place in the 19th century during the Industrial Revolution. People left their homes and work as farmers in the countryside in their thousands and took jobs in factories located in towns and cities. From this time until very recently Britain's urban areas, its towns and cities, have continued to grow as people seek employment that they cannot find in rural areas.

However, in the last thirty years a new pattern has emerged. Many people are now deciding to leave the city and live in the countryside in order to enjoy a better environment. This process is called **counterurbanisation**. Cities have become congested, polluted and blighted by crime and have become expensive and stressful places to live. Many people in Britain, particularly those who have children, have therefore decided to move to villages in rural areas. This has been made increasingly easier in the last thirty years for a number of reasons (see Fig. 4.5.4).

Counterurbanisation has meant that many rural villages have seen significant new house building in recent years and subsequent swelling of their populations. Many villages, with their new housing estates, now look like the suburbs of a city and are therefore called **suburbanised villages**. With higher populations, such villages might have been expected to support more services such as shops, banks and primary schools, but in fact the opposite has occurred. Some services in suburbanised villages have actually decreased because most people in the village are commuters who use the services of the towns and cities they work in rather than supporting the local village services.

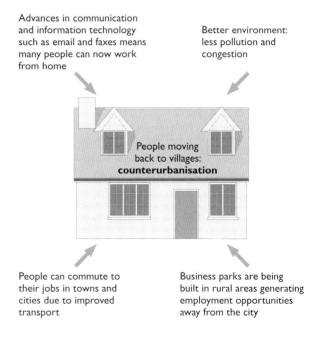

Advances in communication and information technology such as email and faxes means many people can now work from home

Better environment: less pollution and congestion

People moving back to villages: **counterurbanisation**

People can commute to their jobs in towns and cities due to improved transport

Business parks are being built in rural areas generating employment opportunities away from the city

Fig. 4.5.4: Reasons for counterurbanisation in Britain

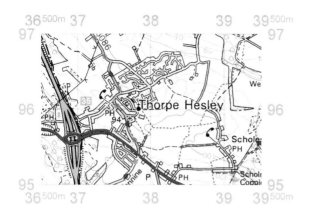

Fig. 4.5.5: OS map extract of Thorpe Hesley

The map above shows the village of Thorpe Hesley near Sheffield which can also be seen on the OS map extract of Sheffield on page 133 at grid square 3796. Thorpe Hesley is a good example of a village that has become suburbanised. It is situated in a rural area but is only 9.5 km (6 miles) from Sheffield, hence people wishing to live in a more rural environment have left Sheffield and relocated there. Thorpe Hesley has grown significantly in the last thirty years and, although it maintains a typical village centre, it is surrounded by new sprawling housing estates. There are no services in Thorpe Hesley as the majority of its population commute to Sheffield and use services such as those found at Meadowhall shopping centre at grid reference 393909.

Although most people living in Thorpe Hesley are commuters, two groups of people in particular may feel isolated in the village due to the lack of services. Elderly people may not have their own transport or may not be in good enough health to travel out of the village to perform vital tasks such as food shopping. Young people such as teenagers may also feel isolated and bored due to the lack of social opportunities in the village which has at times led to petty crime such as vandalism. Both groups may suffer from a feeling of lack of community as there is no social focus around facilities in the village due to their absence.

Summary

Migration is the process of people moving from one place to another and can be voluntary or forced, temporary or permanent.

- The reasons why people leave an area or country are called push factors and commonly include war, drought or unemployment.

- The reasons why people are drawn to move to another area or country are called pull factors and commonly include better education and healthcare or family ties.

LEDCs tend to see a lot of international migration to MEDCs or rural-urban migration. In MEDCs counterurbanisation has become a common process.

Exercise 4I

1. Write sentences to explain the meaning of each of the following words:
   migration   emigrate   immigrant   refugee

2. Why do migrants sometimes have no choice about moving to a different area or country? Try to use example LEDCs in your answer.

3. Why are people living in MEDCs attracted to live abroad, whether temporarily or permanently?

4. Write sentences to explain the meaning of each of the following terms:
   rural-urban migration   counterurbanisation

5. Draw two star diagrams to illustrate, firstly, the reasons why villages are becoming suburbanised and, secondly, the problems this may create.

Exercise 4J

1. Why do you think illegal immigrants risk going to prison in order to live in a country other than their own?

2. How has counterurbanisation affected the function of rural settlements today?

3. Look at the OS map extract of Sheffield on pages 132 and 133. Identify a village other than Thorpe Hesley that may have been suburbanised. How will this have affected different social groups in the community?

Exercise 4K: Enquiry suggestion

To determine whether shops in your nearest settlement are high or low order services, conduct a survey outside selected shops asking customers a series of questions. To start you will need to draw a map of the streets where you will be conducting the survey, for which you may need a local street map or town plan. Identify which shops you wish to stand outside and make predictions as to whether they will be selling convenience or comparison goods. Before you depart, design a questionnaire that will ask customers what they have bought, if they compared the price of the item they bought with prices in any other shop, how often they buy this item and how far they have travelled to buy it. You could add other questions to see which mode of transport they used and why. You will need to ask the permission of the shopkeepers to conduct surveys outside their shops and should conduct the survey with at least one other person. When you return, analyse your results to see if your predictions were correct. Finally, put the shops you have selected into a hierarchy.

Exercise 4L: Past exam questions

1. Many rural settlements are changing. Some are growing, others are declining. Using examples where possible, explain why this is. (6 marks)

2. Look at this sketch map which shows where the different types of shopping centres are located in a town.
    (a) Describe where each of the shopping areas is located. (4 marks)
    (b) Suggest reasons why this pattern of shopping has developed in the town. (8 marks)

3. State two ways in which the urban land use pattern is different in an MEDC from an LEDC. (2 marks)

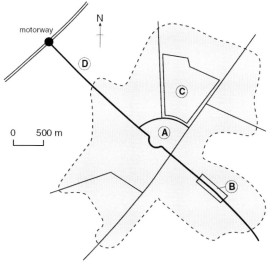

key
- - - edge of built-up area
—— main roads
(A) shopping mall
(B) shopping street
(C) area with corner shops
(D) large superstore

4. Look at the map of this town and describe its site. (2 marks)

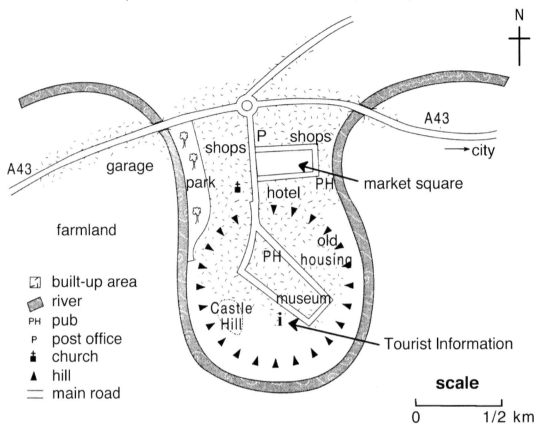

5. Column A below shows services provided in various settlements. Put the following settlements in the right place in column B: **village**; **city**; **town**; **hamlet**.

A	B
Department store, university, airport	
Few scattered houses, no shops	
Primary school, shop, post office	
Secondary school, library, bank	(4 marks)

Exercise 4M: Scholarship or more advanced question
(a) What is the difference between site and situation? (4 marks)

(b) How have rural settlements changed over the last fifty years? (6 marks)

(c) What effect have the changes had on life in rural areas? (9 marks)

(d) What is the future of rural areas? (6 marks)

Exercise 4N
Solve the following clues.

1. Someone who lives in one settlement but travels to work in another (8 letters)
2. Process of people moving either within or between countries (9 letters)
3. Type of informal housing found in LEDCs (6 letters)
4. Opposite to question 8 (5 letters)
5. A type of housing often found in the outer suburbs of the city (8 letters)
6. An old building that has been redeveloped has been… (10 letters)
7. The purpose of a settlement (8 letters)
8. A built-up area – town or city (5 letters)
9. Name given to people who do not settle but move from place to place (7 letters)
10. Settlement pattern found along coasts and valleys (6 letters)

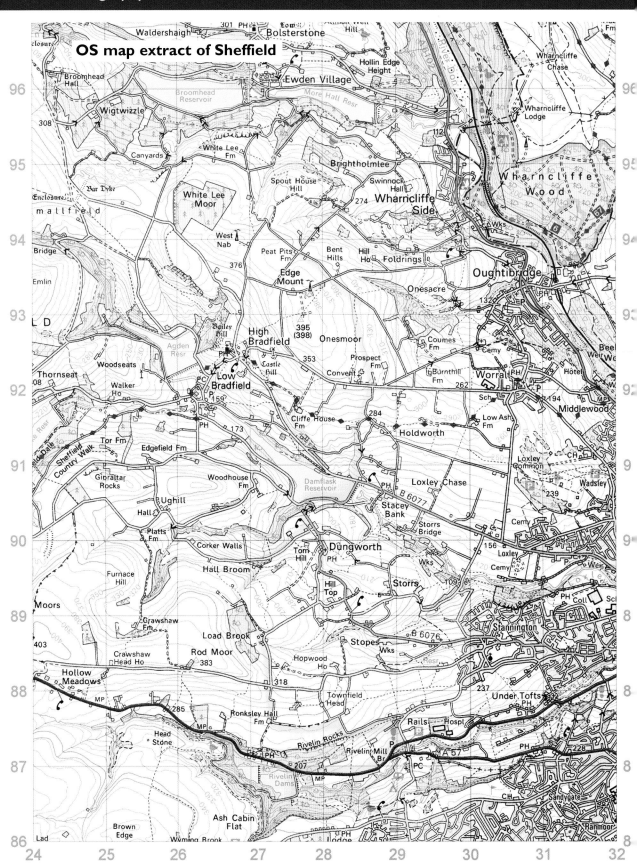

OS map extract of Sheffield

Settlement glossary

Agriculture	Another word for farming.
Arterial road	An important road that links suburbs of the city with the CBD of the city. Usually an 'A' road and often a dual carriageway.
Bypass	A road built around a town.
Catchment area	The area from which people will travel to a shop or service.
Central Business District (CBD)	The centre of a city or town, associated with high rise offices, shops and entertainment facilities.
Commute	To travel to work some distance from where you live.
Comparison goods	Expensive items that people need to compare in price before buying and will travel a long way to buy, such as jewellery, electronic items and clothes.
Conurbation	Large urban area formed from the merging of towns and villages as population has grown and expansion has taken place.
Convenience goods	Cheap goods that people need on a regular basis and will not travel far to buy, such as newspapers, milk and bread.
Counterurbanisation	The process of people moving back to rural areas from the city.
Detached housing	Housing that is within its own grounds, often found in the outer suburbs.
Dispersed settlement	Individual houses or small groups of houses spread thinly across a given area, often found in agricultural or mountainous areas.
Dormitory settlement	A village that has expanded due to a large proportion of its population commuting to larger settlements.
Emigration	The process of people moving abroad permanently.
Floodplain	The flat land either side of a river in lowland that is very good for farming.
Function	The purpose or purposes of a settlement which change and often increase in number over time.

Green belt	A band of countryside surrounding a city in which urban growth is regulated to prevent the city spreading.
Hierarchy	A chart (often a pyramid) ranking settlements by their size and the number of services they have.
High order service	Shops selling comparison (high order) goods. High order goods cost a lot but are not bought very often, such as electronic items.
Illegal immigrant	Somebody who has entered another country for work or better living standards without permission.
Immigrant	Somebody who has moved permanently to a different country.
Industrial Revolution	A period of history when people left the countryside to work in factories in towns and cities.
Inner city	Land use zone of the city which has a lot of terraced housing.
Inner suburbs	Land use zone of the city which has a lot of semi-detached housing.
International migration	The movement of people to another country to seek work, health and social benefits.
Land use	What is built upon a piece of land.
LEDC	Less Economically Developed Country.
Linear settlement	Houses and buildings arranged in a line along a road, river, valley bottom, etc. See Ribbon settlement.
Low order service	Shops selling convenience (low order) goods. Low order goods cost less than high order goods but are bought more regularly, such as food.
MEDC	More Economically Developed Country.
Migration	The movement of people from one area to another seeking work, health and social benefits.
Model	A simplified view of how cities in general are split into different zones.
Modernised	Rebuilt or refurbished.

Nomadic	Term describing early populations that hunted and gathered food so did not settle in one place.
Nucleated settlement	Buildings and houses that are arranged in a circular manner around a crossroads, castle, market place, etc.
Outer suburbs	Land use zone of the city which has a variety of different purposes and is often surrounded by a ring road.
Physical landscape	The natural features of an area such as trees, rivers and mountains.
Plan view	Looking at something as if from above.
Planned settlements	Houses and buildings built from scratch in a well planned ordered form.
Pull factors	Factors that attract migrants to come to an area such as education, medical and social services.
Push factors	Factors that make migrants want to move away from their local area or country such as political fears, war and poor standards of living.
Range	The distance people will travel to a certain shop.
Refugees	People who have been forced to migrate within a country or from one country to another.
Relief	Physical aspects of the land such as height, gradient, aspect.
Ribbon settlement	Houses and buildings arranged in a line along a road, river, valley bottom, etc. See Linear settlement.
Rural	A place that is predominately in the countryside.
Rural-urban migration	People moving from the countryside to the city.
Semi-detached housing	Houses that are joined to another house on one side only, often found in the inner suburbs.
Services	Facilities available in a settlement such as shops or cinemas.
Settlement	A place where people live.

Settlement pattern	The shape of a settlement (linear/nucleated/dispersed).
Shanty town	A rapidly growing, unplanned collection of self-made houses, often with no running water, electricity or proper sanitation.
Site	The specific location of a settlement originally as a result of physical factors such as proximity to a river, etc.
Site factors	The specific reasons why settlers chose a site, such as water supply or defence.
Situation	The location of a settlement in relation to its surrounding area.
Subsistence farming	When a farmer produces just enough food for his family to eat.
Suburb	A band of housing on the edge of a city.
Suburbanised village	A village in which the number of houses has grown due to increased commuting. It therefore has some resemblance to the suburbs of a city.
Surplus	Another word for extra or spare.
Terraced housing	Rows of houses that are joined together, often found in the inner city.
Threshold	The minimum population of a settlement to support a shop.
Urbanisation	The increase in percentage of people living in cities.
Urban	A place that is mainly covered by buildings such as a town or city.
Urban renewal	Improving the buildings and the environment of an urban area.
Urban sprawl	The continued outward growth of cities. Sometimes limited by the green belt.

Chapter 5: Location knowledge

A satellite image of the world

Location knowledge is your knowledge of where places are in the world. At the beginning of the Common Entrance exam there is a specific 'location knowledge' section which is worth roughly 15% of the marks on the paper. It is useful therefore to learn all the information in this chapter well, so you do not waste time pondering where to plot a capital city or trying to think of the name of a river. This chapter will teach you the following:

- The location of the world's major physical features, such as continents and mountain ranges.

- The location of the imaginary lines plotted on the globe such as the Equator and the tropics of Cancer and Capricorn.

- The location of the physical features of Britain that you need to know for the exam.

- The name, location and capital city of countries in each continent.

- The location of other major cities across the globe.

- How to revise location knowledge information for the exam.

5.1 The world's major physical features

What you need to know

Location knowledge requires you to be able to name and place many of the world's well known physical features. Such features include the world's continents, oceans and important rivers and mountain ranges. You will find a detailed list of exactly what you need to know below. Figs. 5.1.1 (below), and 5.1.2 and 5.1.3 on page 140 illustrate this information on a world base map. It is very easy to think you know this basic information about the world's physical features but make sure you can locate accurately all the physical features listed below otherwise you may lose easy marks in this part of the exam.

Continents: Africa, Antarctica, Asia, Oceania, Europe, North and South America

Oceans: Arctic, Indian, North and South Atlantic, Pacific, Southern

Mountain ranges: Alps, Andes, Himalayas, Pyrenees, Rocky Mountains

Deserts: Sahara

Rivers: Amazon, Mississippi, Nile, Rhine, Yangtze

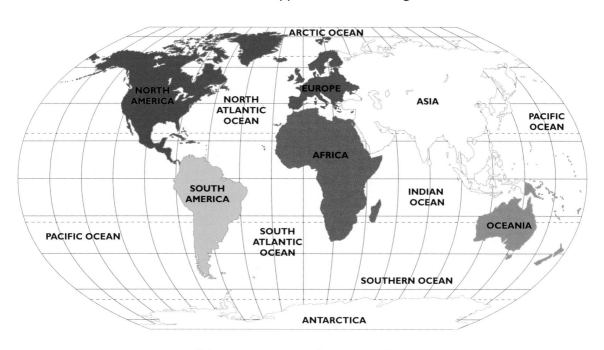

© Lewis continental colour coding, 2005

Fig. 5.1.1: Continents and oceans

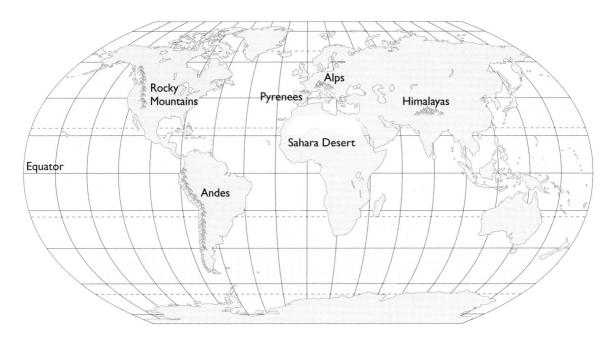

Fig. 5.1.2: Mountain ranges and deserts

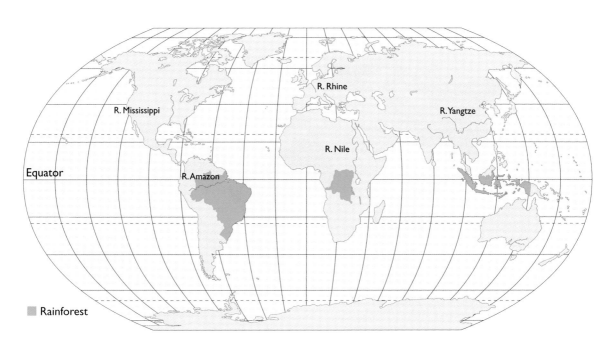

Fig. 5.1.3: Rivers and tropical forests

How an exam will test your knowledge

Most questions testing location knowledge in an exam require short answers and are based on an atlas-style map of Britain, the world or any of the continents.

There are basically two methods that could be employed in an exam to test that you know where the world's major physical features are located.

- There may be letters on the map you are provided with and you will be expected to name, for example, the mountain range marked A or the river marked B.

- You may be asked to plot the location of, for example, the Sahara Desert.

When plotting information on a map be sure to be accurate and clear, to avoid losing marks. Use a sharp pencil, so that if you make a mistake you can correct it. If you are shading an area to represent a desert or mountain range remember that the area you cover needs to be accurate, particularly when it comes to crossing international borders. Look at Figs. 5.1.4 and 5.1.5 below. They show a good way and bad way of answering the question 'shade and label the Alps mountain range on the map of Europe'. Notice the differences between the strong and weak answer. The strong answer is spelt correctly, shades the correct area, crossing the correct international borders and uses a straight line to indicate where the label refers to. This makes the labelling neat and is particularly useful if more than one feature has to be labelled on the same map. The shading should be in pencil.

Fig. 5.1.4: Strong answer   *Fig. 5.1.5: Weak answer*

When labelling continents, countries or physical features, spell accurately and keep your writing to a reasonably small size; you have no idea what else you may yet need to label in that space. Arrows are a useful way of labelling features without using up valuable space.

Exam tip

Use Fig. 5.1.1 to Fig. 5.1.3 (pages 139–140) or an atlas to check that you know the exact location of all the major world physical features you are required to know for your exam. Use blank maps of Britain, Europe and the world to plot all the physical features. Blank maps are available for download from the Galore Park website www.galorepark.co.uk

Repeat this process several times before your exam so you know the information by heart. You could colour the maps and put them on your bedroom walls as a revision aid.

Summary

The location knowledge section of an exam requires you to learn a large amount of information about where places are located in the world. This can seem a lot to learn but it can be broken down into smaller sections which are more manageable. In this section of location knowledge you are required to learn about the world's continents, oceans, mountain ranges, deserts and rivers.

Level 1   Exercise 5A

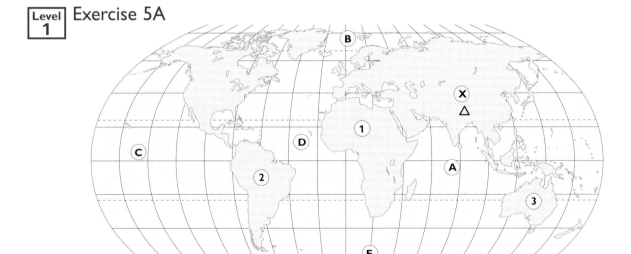

Fig. 5.1.6: Test map

1. Name the seven continents.

2. Look at the map above. Match each of the letters A to E with the name of an ocean.

3. Look at the map above. Which number represents the Sahara Desert?

Level
2

Exercise 5B

1. List the mountain ranges you need to know and which continents they are in.

2. List the rivers you need to know and name the seas or oceans they flow into.

3. The △ represents the world's tallest mountain, Everest, in mountain range **X**. What is the name of mountain range **X**?

5.2 The British Isles

What you need to know

From time to time the location knowledge aspect of an exam will be based on a map of Britain and will test your knowledge of the different physical features of the British Isles such as important rivers, mountain ranges and sea areas. However, you also need to know about human features such as the location of national borders as well as major cities and towns. You will find a detailed list of exactly what you need to know on page 144. The figures 5.2.1 and 5.2.2 on page 144 illustrate this information on British Isles base maps. It is very easy to think you know this basic information about Britain's features but make sure you can locate accurately all the features shown below otherwise you may lose easy marks in this part of an exam.

Fig. 5.2.1: The British Isles: physical features

Fig. 5.2.2: The British Isles: cities and country borders

Countries: UK, Republic of Ireland

Sea areas: English Channel, Irish Sea, North Sea

Rivers: Severn, Thames, Trent, Clyde, Shannon

Mountains/hills: Grampians, North West Highlands, Pennines, Lake District, Snowdonia

Major cities: Belfast, Birmingham, Cardiff, Dublin, Edinburgh, Glasgow, Liverpool, London, Manchester, Newcastle

How an exam will test your knowledge

Much of the advice given in the previous section applies when answering and plotting information about the British Isles on a blank base map. Again you could be asked to name, for example, the river marked A or the sea area marked B. You are more likely to be asked to draw and label on a base map of the British Isles. You may need to sketch in and label a lot of information so even greater accuracy and neatness is necessary.

It is important to remember that the British Isles is essentially comprised of two sets of isles: the United Kingdom and the Republic of Ireland. Great Britain is the name given to the three nations of England, Wales and Scotland. Together with Northern Ireland, this comprises the United Kingdom. It is useful to know where the borders are between these nations and be able to draw them onto a base map of the British Isles.

Exam tip

Use Figs. 5.2.1 and 5.2.2 (pages 143–144) or an atlas to check that you know the exact location of all the major physical features of the British Isles you are required to know for your exam. Don't forget you also need to know the location of human features such as the major cities. Use blank maps of Britain to plot all the physical features and human features. Repeat this process several times before your exam so you know the information by heart. You could colour the maps and put them on your bedroom walls as a revision aid.

Summary

The location knowledge aspect of an exam requires you to learn a large amount of information about where places are located in the world. This can seem a lot to learn but it can be broken down into smaller sections which are more manageable. In this section of location knowledge you are required to learn about the country boundaries, major cities, rivers, sea areas, hills and mountains of the British Isles.

Exercise 5C

Fig. 5.2.3: Test map

Referring to the figure above:

1. Name the three rivers marked A, B and C.

2. Name the port cities that are marked A, B and C on the map.

3. Which is the correct border between England and Scotland: line X, Y or Z?

Exercise 5D

Again refer to Fig. 5.2.3 above.

1. Name the cities marked D, E, F, G and H.

2. (a) Which is the correct national border of Northern Ireland: 1, 2 or 3?
   (b) Which country does Northern Ireland border?

3. Name the mountainous area marked V and the mountain range marked W.

5.3 Countries and cities

What you need to know

This is the largest part of the location knowledge section. You will find lists of exactly what you need to know on the pages that follow. Figs. 5.3.1, 5.3.2 and 5.3.3 also illustrate this information.

European countries and their capitals

EU members		**Non EU members**	
France	Paris	Switzerland	Berne*
Germany	Berlin	Ukraine	Kiev*
Greece	Athens*		
Italy	Rome		
Poland	Warsaw		
Spain	Madrid		
Sweden	Stockholm*		
United Kingdom	London		
Czech Republic*	Prague*		

It can be straightforward to learn the capitals of the European countries within the syllabus, but you must remember that you also need to be able to recognise each country should its borders be drawn on a base map and be able to plot where the capital city is within its country. (*These are not required for Common Entrance).

Fig. 5.3.1: European countries and their capitals

World countries

You need to be able to identify the following world countries and be able to plot them on a world map (see Fig. 5.3.2).

Africa
Egypt
Ethiopia
Kenya
Nigeria
South Africa

Americas
Brazil
Canada
Mexico
USA

Asia
Afghanistan
Bangladesh
China
India
Indonesia
Iran
Iraq
Japan
Pakistan
Russia
Saudi Arabia

Oceania
Australia
New Zealand

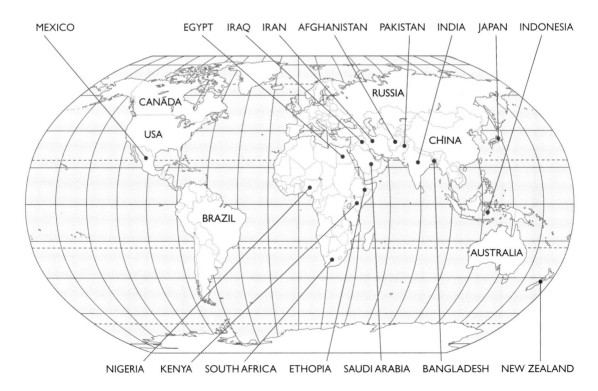

Fig. 5.3.2: World countries

Major cities

You will also need to be able to plot on any given base map the exact location of the following major cities. These are important cities but are not necessarily the capitals of their countries. You will find these cities plotted on Fig. 5.3.3 and listed below.

Beijing (China)

Cairo (Egypt)

Delhi (India)

Los Angeles (USA)

Mexico City (Mexico)

Moscow (Russia)

New York (USA)

Rio de Janeiro (Brazil)

Sydney (Australia)

Tokyo (Japan)

Washington DC (USA)

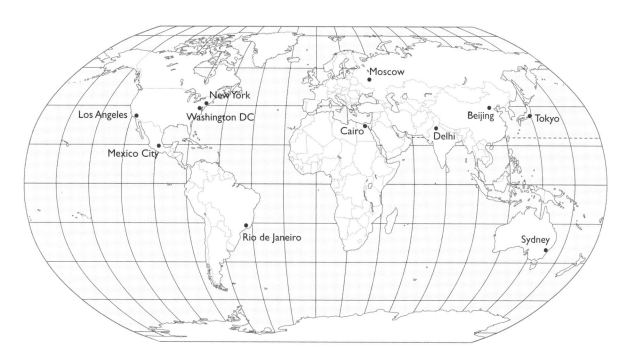

Fig. 5.3.3: Major cities

How an exam will test your knowledge

Most commonly you will be asked to identify countries or cities marked by letters on a base map of either Europe or the world. If you are asked to shade and label a country on a base map, make sure you draw the borders of the country accurately, shade the country neatly and label it carefully. If you are asked to plot a city on a map, be sure to plot it accurately and spell it correctly.

Exam tip

It is important to learn the cities and countries that are listed. This is best learnt by having a friend or member of your family test you on them regularly and maybe by keeping a list on your bedroom wall at home. Use Figs. 5.3.1, 5.3.2 and 5.3.3 or an atlas to check you know the location of all the countries and cities that you are required to know. Don't forget you must be able to identify the borders of these countries. Use blank maps of Europe and the world (available for download from the Galore Park website www.galorepark.co.uk) to plot all the countries and cities you need to know. Repeat this process several times before your exam so you know the information by heart. You could colour the maps and put them on your bedroom walls as a revision aid.

Alternatively, create a number of index cards, with an outline map of a given country on each. Mark the exact location of any cities that you are required to know and any further information, including physical features, you need to learn that are located in this county such as rivers or mountains. It is a good idea to list this information on the reverse of each index card.

Summary

The location knowledge aspect of an exam requires you to learn a large amount of information about where places are located in the world. This can seem a lot to learn but it can be broken down into smaller sections which are more manageable. In this section of location knowledge you are required to learn the location of selected countries in each of the continents, their borders/boundaries and some major cities.

Exercise 5E

1. Look at Fig. 5.3.4. Name the countries marked A, B, C, D and E.

2. Look at Fig. 5.3.4. Name the capital city of countries A, B, C, D and E.

3. Look at Fig. 5.3.5, on page 152. Which of the countries marked X, Y and Z is Kenya?

Fig. 5.3.4: Countries and capitals European test map

Exercise 5F

1. Look at Fig. 5.3.4.
    (a) Name the country marked F.
    (b) Name the capital city of the country marked F.
    (c) Is the capital city located at point 1 or 2 with country F?

2. Look at Fig. 5.3.5 on page 152. If you travelled in a straight line from the countries labelled as 3 and 4 you would cross five countries. Name these countries.

3. Look at Fig. 5.3.5:
   (a) Name the country marked 1 on the world map.
   (b) Name the country marked 2 on the world map.
   (c) Name the two countries that border country 2.

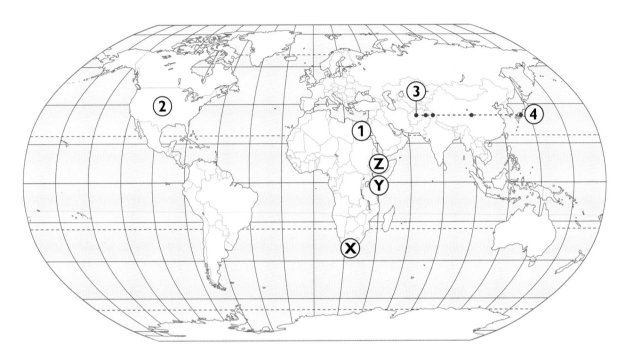

Fig. 5.3.5: Countries and capitals world test map

Level
2

Exercise 5G

Look at Fig. 5.3.6:

1. Name the following world cities labelled and located in North America.
    (a) 1
    (b) 2

2. Name the following world cities labelled and located in Central and South America.
    (a) 3
    (b) 4

3. Name the following world cities labelled and located in Asia.
    (a) 5
    (b) 6

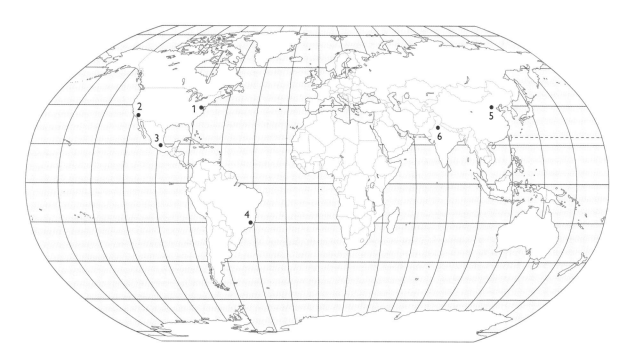

Fig. 5.3.6: Cites world test map

5.4 Other features of the globe

What you need to know

There are several other pieces of information that you need to know for the location knowledge section of a syllabus. The information you need to know is shown on the world map below.

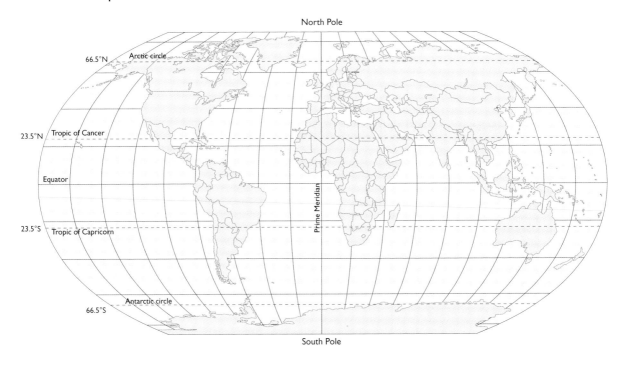

Fig. 5.4.1: Other features of the globe

You must be able to recognise, and possibly plot on a world base map, five different lines of latitude. Lines of latitude are the imaginary lines that run around the globe horizontally. The Equator is the line of latitude that runs round the centre of the globe and is given a value of 0°. From the Equator the North Pole is at a 90 degree angle or bearing, so we say the North Pole is 90° north. The South Pole is also at a 90 degree bearing from the Equator, so we say the South Pole is 90° south. You need to be able to plot the location of the North and South Poles.

In between the Equator and the poles are four other lines of latitude. These are the Tropic of Cancer at 23.5° north, the Arctic Circle at 66.5° north, the Tropic of Capricorn at 23.5° south and the Antarctic Circle at 66.5° south.

The imaginary lines that run around the globe vertically are called lines of longitude. You must be able to identify on a world base map only two different lines of longitude. Firstly, the Prime Meridian (also called the Greenwich Meridian) which is given a value of 0° and which runs from the North Pole to the South Pole through London. Secondly, the International Date Line which runs from the North Pole to the South Pole on the other side of the globe to the Prime Meridian and has a value of 180° (see Fig. 5.4.2).

Lines of longitude combined with national borders determine the time zones of the world. The sun rises to the east of the International Date Line and sets to the west of it. This means that as you travel east of Britain you have to put your watch forwards. If you travel to the west of Britain you have to put your watch backwards.

Fig. 5.4.2: The International Date Line

How an exam will test your knowledge

You will not be asked to draw lines of latitude or longitude onto a base map but you are likely to be asked to identify unlabelled lines such as the Equator or the International Date Line. Be sure to label these lines in clear but small letters on a base map as you may need to add further information in questions that follow.

Summary

This section of the location knowledge topic requires you to learn the names of five lines of latitude and two lines of longitude including their values in degrees.

Exercise 5H

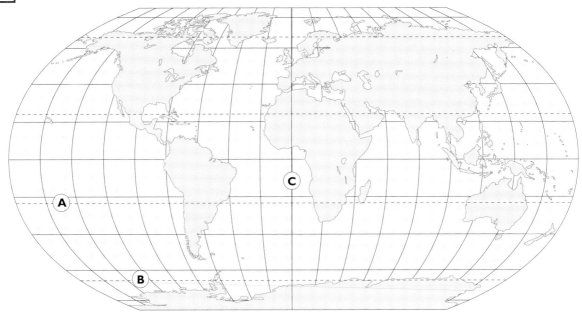

Fig. 5.4.3: Other features of the globe and other world cities test map

Referring to the world map above answer the following:
1. (a) Name the line of latitude marked A.
    (b) What is the value of this line in degrees?

2. (a) Name the line of latitude marked B.
    (b) What is the value of this line in degrees?

3. (a) Name the line of longitude marked C.
    (b) What is the value of this line in degrees?

Exercise 5I: Enquiry suggestion
To help learn all the information for the location knowledge section of the exam why not make it interesting by creating a game? There are many different quiz shows; you could choose the same format as one of the popular quiz shows and create questions based on the information you have to learn. If you and your friends created different types of quiz you could try them out on each other, maybe with the help of your Geography teacher, and improve your location knowledge and have fun while you are doing it!

Exercise 5J: Past exam questions

The following questions are taken from recent past papers. You will be asked to label features on a world base map which you can download from the Galore Park website www.galorepark.co.uk

Look at the world map below.

1. Name the countries marked A, B and C on the world map. (3 marks)

2. Name the mountain ranges marked X, Y and Z on the world map. (3 marks)

3. On a world map, mark and name the following cities:
    (a) Beijing (1 mark)
    (b) Washington DC (1 mark)
    (c) Madrid (1 mark)

4. If you fly east from Canada to France,
    (a) which ocean will you cross? (1 mark)
    (b) will you put your watch forward or back? (1 mark)

5. (a) What is the name of the tropic which passes through Egypt? (1 mark)
    (b) What is the capital of Egypt? (1 mark)
    (c) What is the name of the river which flows through Egypt? (1 mark)

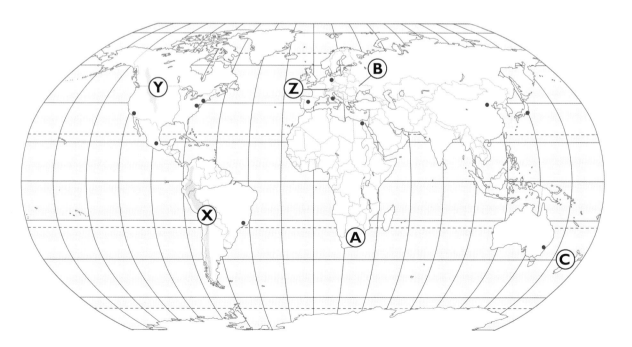

Exercise 5K: Location knowledge summary crossword

Solve the following clues.

1. Capital city of Poland (6 letters)
2. Irish river (7 letters)
3. South American mountain range (5 letters)
4. Mountainous area in north of Wales (9 letters)
5. Country to the east of China (5 letters)
6. Capital city of Afghanistan (5 letters)
7. African river which flows through Egypt (4 letters)
8. Capital city of India: New . . . . (5 letters)
9. City in the north west of England (10 letters)
10. American river that flows into the Gulf of Mexico (11 letters)

Chapter 6: Essential exam technique

Taking an exam

Many pupils are disappointed by their performance in practice exams. This is often because they have revised the Geography topics well but have been let down by poor exam technique. This chapter will help you with this essential aspect of doing well in the Geography exam by:

- Explaining how the Geography paper is structured and what type of questions will be posed.

- Showing you where the majority of marks are available and for what skills or knowledge they are given.

- Showing what command words could be used in questions and how to respond to them.

- Advising you on what mistakes are often made in the exam and how to avoid them.

- Illustrating examples of strong and weak answers.

6.1 The Common Entrance Examination

The structure of the exam

The style of the 2010 Geography (Common Entrance) CE paper has a very different format to the past papers that you may have seen or used to practise your skills and knowledge. This style of paper reflects a significant change in the syllabus with a shift towards a greater need for pupils to be able to apply skills they have developed throughout the course. Although there is no longer a dedicated case study section in the CE paper detailed examples will be required in section C of the exam where the following topics will be tested: landform processes, weather and climate, environmental issues, economic activity. These examples are highlighted in both *So you really want to learn Geography* books as 'syllabus examples'.

The exam is in three parts: Section A (15 marks), Section B (15 marks) and Section C (50 marks). The fieldwork project is worth 20 marks. The table below shows the areas covered in each part of the exam and the *So you really want to learn Geography* textbook in which each subject is covered.

Section A: Location knowledge (15 marks)

Location knowledge	Books 1 and 2

Section B: OS mapwork (15 marks)

OS mapwork	Books 1 and 2

Section C: Thematic studies (50 marks)

1. Landform processes	Book 2
2. Weather and climate	Book 2
3. Settlement	Book 2
4. Economic activity	Book 1
5. Environmental issues	Book 1

Shorter answer questions

Question focus and format

Most questions in the exam require you to write a couple of lines to explain and answer. This style of question demands knowledge and skills from a wide variety of topics that you will have studied in class and more skills based on data response type questions. There are typically around five separate questions, each with several parts, in section C of the exam. Questions are layered in that they may offer one or two opening questions where only a few marks are awarded for identifying physical feature or demonstrating a map skill (see Fig. 6.1.1).

Remember that the Ordnance Survey map that comes with the exam paper will be at either a 1:25 000 or 1:50 000 scale. There will be a scale ratio on the bottom of the map and a full key to tell you what all the map symbols mean. Although a key is provided, it helps to know the common map symbols (tourist information centre/campsite/train station, etc) so that you spend less time on any mapwork question and have more time for the more valuable second layer questions.

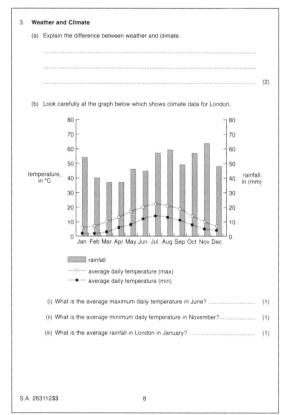

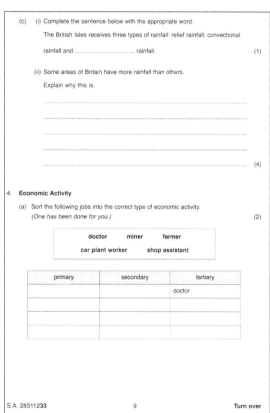

Fig. 6.1.1: Section C layered question

Essential exam tip!

Look at how marks are allocated in your practice papers. This should help you identify the skills and knowledge that you need to practise and revise for the exam. Stay calm if you seem to be taking a while to complete mapwork questions only worth 1 or 2 marks; don't get stuck in a rut. If you are having real trouble with a certain question or skill, move on and come back to it at the end of the paper.

Data sources and drawing diagrams

Often a source of data accompanies a question. This could be a map, a photograph, a table, a graph or a diagram. If this is the case, examine the data carefully before trying to answer the question. If there are figures available, use them to support your answer. For example, there may be a map of Britain showing temperature differences between different regions. The question may ask you to give an explanation for these differences. In your answer you should, of course, give an explanation, but also refer to figures on the map.

Other questions require you to draw diagrams. You may be asked, for example, to explain how the processes of freeze-thaw weathering occur or how a waterfall on a river is formed. In this case you will either be given a large box in which to draw your diagrams, or a smaller box with lines below for you to write an explanation of what you have drawn in the box. In both cases, but particularly when there is nowhere for a written explanation, it is vital that you add detailed labels to explain the processes occurring. A series of small diagrams can often explain the stages of a process more clearly than one big diagram.

Essential exam tip!

Location knowledge questions often demand that you name or plot location knowledge information using an outline map provided with the paper. When plotting information on an outline map be sure to be accurate and clear to avoid losing marks. Always use pencil in case you have misinterpreted the question and need to rub out your answer.

Longer answer questions – syllabus example questions based on specific aspects of the topics you have studied

Question focus and format

The final layer of a question may carry the highest number of marks and will ask you about a syllabus example (case study) you have studied in class. There are case studies for the following topics: tectonic processes, landform processes, economic activities and environmental issues.

If you have used both *So you really want to learn Geography* textbooks while studying for Geography CE you will be well prepared to answer any section C question. Within each chapter of both books, case studies that can be discussed in this section of the exam are clearly indicated by the subtitle syllabus example. All case studies within these books begin with an explanation of the theory concerning the case study, followed by a factual explanation of what happened, often analysing the consequences within the categories of immediate and then long-term effects.

Common mistakes

Ordnance Survey mapwork

Four and six figure grid references

You should have learnt the rules that apply to this skill in class but under pressure it is easy to forget that you always read or use the easting (bottom) figure first then the northing (side) figure last. As with all skills, practice makes perfect and eliminates mistakes.

Accuracy

Giving a rough or inaccurate answer could lose you some or all of the marks in a mapwork question that asks you, for example, to measure the distance along a road using the scale, or to measure the height increase up a slope using contour lines. A few seconds checking your answer and making sure it is correct could get you the vital marks you need. Taking string into the exam will mean measuring windy routes is quick and easy. Simply lay the string along the route and then straighten it out to measure it, referring to the scale on the map.

Shorter and longer answer questions

Technical terms

During your classes in the years leading up to the Common Entrance Geography exam, you will have come across many of the technical terms that will be used in the exam questions. If you do not understand the meaning of a word or words in a question, you will not be able to answer it, even if you know everything about that topic. How frustrating! For example here is a question used in a previous paper.

'Look at the OS extract. Describe the ways in which *conflicting economic demands* may have affected the *environment* shown on the map.'

You may understand how the wildlife and local people can be affected by the growth of different industries (which is what the question is asking) but you may not understand one or more of the words in italics, preventing you from answering the question well, if at all. Both *So you really want to learn Geography* textbooks highlight such **key terms** within the text and explain their meaning in the glossary at the end of the chapter. To help you further, study the command words that examiners use in the exam questions (Appendix 2, page 180) and the syllabus glossary (available for download from Galore Park website www.galorepark.co.uk).

Essential exam tip!
As well as learning the meaning of key terms so that you can understand the question, it is also a good idea to use these terms in your answers to get the highest mark possible.

Identifying your mistakes
The mistakes mentioned so far happen often and are made, to some degree, by all students. However, your teacher will probably give you plenty of past examination paper questions as practice questions, and you will complete one or two mock exam papers before doing the real thing in the summer. It is a really good idea to keep all these practice questions and papers and look through them when revising to see if you can identify any of the mistakes discussed above, or any mistake that you have made more than once. Learn from your mistakes and improve your exam technique.

Location knowledge
The few mistakes that are made with these questions are a result of rushing and inaccuracy, as they are at the end of the paper and time is all too often running out. The best way to avoid mistakes is simply to learn everything you need to know (see Chapter 5). When you are asked to plot a city, desert, mountain range or similar on the map it is important to plot it clearly and accurately. The advice is simple: learn it!

Reading exam questions
Here is some general advice that applies to all parts of the paper. It is advice you have heard before and will hear again, and there is a reason for this! It is absolutely essential that you read the instructions on the front of the paper, know what to do and how long you have to do it. The exam in its present form is one hour long and you have to answer all the questions. Always read the question carefully, twice to be sure, especially where it is worth several marks. Just as important is to make sure you do answer the question. Look for key words or terms in the question to identify what it wants from you.

Examples of strong and weak answers

To help you produce good answers to questions we will now illustrate what constitutes a strong and a weak answer to the same question using two past paper questions. The shorter answer example question is based on the topic of tectonic processes and refers to a world map showing how the world is split up into tectonic plates. The longer answer example question is based on the topic of environmental issues and refers to the OS map in that particular paper which was centred on a National Park. For both questions we have given a strong answer and explained why it is good, and a weak answer and explained why it is poor. Notice the differences between the quality of the strong and weak answers. Look at past papers or test questions you have done, then identify which answers are strong and which are weak.

Shorter answer example question

Explain why the distribution of earthquakes and volcanoes are so similar. Use the information from the map to support your answer. (5 marks – 8 lines)

Strong answer

Earthquakes and volcanoes both occur on plate boundaries. There are four different types of plate boundary. A constructive boundary where plates move apart such as the American and Eurasian plates which create new islands like Sertsey near Iceland shown on the map. Destructive plate boundaries where oceanic plates go under continental, creating earthquakes and volcanoes such as the Andes mountains. Conservative boundaries, such as the San Andreas fault, USA shown on the map, where two plates slide past each other causing earthquakes. Finally collision boundaries where two continental plates push together creating mountain ranges such as the Himalayas.

Why it is a strong answer

- It immediately answers the question – *earthquakes and volcanoes both occur on plate boundaries.*

- It goes further to show the candidate's understanding of the different types of plate boundaries.

- It seeks extra marks by referring to specific examples.

- It refers to the data source (the world map showing how the world is split into tectonic plates) on at least two occasions, as suggested in the question.

Weak answer

Earthquakes happen on plates and are spread across the world. In America there was a big earthquake that killed lots of people and they now make special buildings that are earthquake proof.

Why it is a weak answer

- It does not answer the question. The pupil needed to say that earthquakes and volcanoes occur at specific places which are called plate boundaries. They are not spread evenly across the world.

- It only talks about earthquakes when the question asked about the distribution of earthquakes and volcanoes.

- It vaguely discusses an example but this is an irrelevant one that is lacking any statistics to back it up.

- At no point does it refer to the map as suggested in the question.

- It does not use the eight lines available on the paper for the answer.

Longer answer example question

With reference to examples you have studied, describe the ways in which tourists affect the natural environment of scenic areas, such as the one on the map, and explain what has been done to address these problems. (8 marks – 18 lines)

Strong answer

Tourists have damaged the environment in the Peak District National Park in many ways. Over 17 million people live within 60 miles of the Park concentrated in large urban areas such as Manchester, Nottingham and Sheffield with good access to the Park (M1/M6). This means most visitors arrive by car which causes high levels of air pollution as well as causing traffic congestion, both of which are significantly worse in the summer when over 10 000 cars per day use the Park's narrow roads. The activities tourists come to enjoy can also cause damage to the landscape and wildlife creating conflict with the farmers who own most of the land. Walkers often cause soil erosion by not keeping to footpaths, leave farmers' gates open or damage their walls by scrambling over them. More energetic activities such as hang-gliding and mountain biking can frighten wildlife or farmers' livestock and damage delicate vegetation which forms the habitat for species of wild birds.

In an attempt to reduce the levels of pollution and congestion created by visitors arriving by car the Peak District National Park Authority have introduced park and ride schemes which allow tourists to arrive on the borders of the Park by car but then use public transport within the Park. To reduce the conflict that occurs between tourists and farmers the National Park Authority have clearly marked footpaths with signposts, provided separate mountain biking trails to prevent further soil erosion and created specially designated areas for hang-gliding.

Why it is a strong answer

- It immediately introduces an example, as is asked for in the question, to base the rest of the answer upon.

- It gives details of not just one but several ways in which tourists affect the natural environment, referring to specific facts learnt from a case study.

- It goes on to discuss how visitors create conflict not only with the needs of the wildlife in the National Park but also with the interests of local people, in this case farmers.

- It clearly answers the second part of the question which seeks solutions to the problems created by tourism by identifying specific ways in which the National Park Authority have dealt with the problems identified earlier in the question.

Weak answer

Tourism is bad because people litter everywhere and that harms animals which people want to come and see in the first place. I don't think that people should be allowed to drop litter and should be fined if they do in a National Park.

Why it is a weak answer

- It does not use facts and figures from a specific example or examples, as required in the question.

- It only talks about one way in which tourists affect the environment which limits marks.

- It gives a personal opinion in the first person (*I don't think that people should be allowed to drop litter…*) about a solution to problems facing the environment, which is not what the question is asking for.

- It fails to use the eighteen lines available to answer this question.

6.2 The Common Academic Scholarship Examination

The structure of the exam

The CASE paper requires candidates to answer two questions in 60 minutes; one from a choice of two in Section A and one from a choice of around six in Section B. There are six thematic topics within the Geography syllabus, all of which could be tested in the exam. These topics are listed in the table below, which also shows the Galore Park textbook in which each topic is covered.

Section A: Data-response questions (25 marks)

Question 1	Physical and environmental topics
Theme	*So you really want to learn Geography*
Landform processes	Book 2
Weather and climate	Book 2
Tectonic processes	Book 1
Environmental issues	Book 1

Question 2	Human topics
Theme	*So you really want to learn Geography*
Settlement	Book 2
Economic activity	Book 1

Section B: Essay and structured essay questions (25 marks)

Questions based on any of the six physical, environmental and human topics covered in Section A, but the thematic topic focus of the two Section A questions is unlikely to be repeated in any of the Section B questions. Fieldwork investigations may also form the question focus of one of the Section B questions. Fieldwork projects do not directly count towards the CASE mark.

Essential CASE exam tip!

At the top of the CASE paper you are advised to spend approximately 35 minutes answering the Section A question, leaving 25 minutes available for the Section B question. As Section B questions require an essay-style answer you may find 25 minutes is insufficient time, thus it is suggested that candidates spend no more than 30 minutes on Section A, giving adequate time to plan and write a suitable essay answer in Section B.

Section A questions – data-response questions

Question focus and format

As you can see from the information on page 168, this section of the paper carries half of the marks and demands knowledge from all six thematic topics in the CASE syllabus. Question 1 will be based on a physical or environmental topic and question 2 will be based on a human topic. Both questions however are of a data-response style meaning you will have to analyse, interpret and discuss one or more pieces of information provided with the question. This could be a map, a photograph, a table, a graph or a diagram. Examine the data carefully before trying to answer the question and see if you can express your knowledge within all parts of the question by drawing information from the data to illustrate your answer.

Section A questions are layered into three or four parts with more marks being awarded to the latter parts of the question (see Fig. 6.2.1 page 170). You can see the pattern of marks in this question which roughly indicates how much you should write and how long you should spend on each part of the question. Parts (a) and (b) of this question must be answered using the candidate's knowledge of the subject but need to refer to the information in the data sources, particularly to the facts that make up resource A. The next layer of the question, part (c), does not necessarily demand candidates refer to the data sources but goes on to offer considerably more marks for a higher level explanation of a hazard that you will have studied within the six thematic topics of the syllabus.

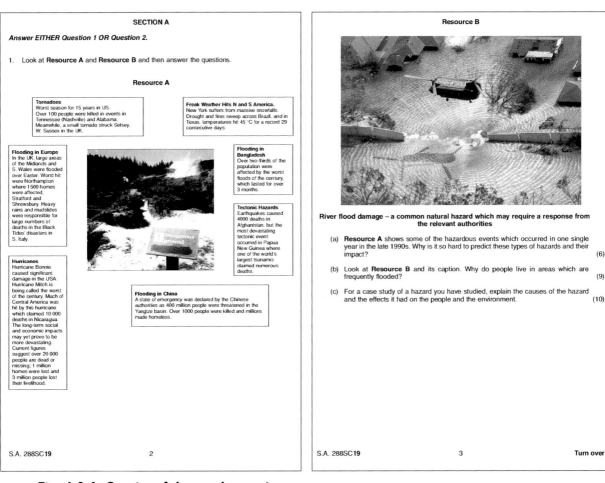

Fig. 6.2.1: Section A layered question

Essential CASE tip!

Look at how marks are allocated in Section A of your practice papers. This should help you to identify what you need to include in different parts of Section A questions and subsequently what you need to revise before you take the exam.

Section B questions – essay and structured essay questions

Question focus and format

As you can see from the information on page 168, this section of the paper also carries half the marks available. There will be around six questions in Section B based on all six thematic topics in the CASE syllabus, as well as the possibility of a question based on fieldwork investigations candidates may have carried out in the years leading up to the exam. As well as a range of questions based on differing thematic topics to choose from, candidates will also be presented with two different styles of questions.

Structured essay questions are similar in format to those in Section A in that they may have three of four parts that relate to each other. However, the mark value for each part can vary significantly so do not be fooled into thinking you will do well on this type of question unless you have looked at each part of the question carefully and decided how you will answer it and whether you can provide enough information to justify the mark value of that part. Look at Fig. 6.2.2 below which is an example of this sort of structured essay question. Notice that part (b) is worth twice as many marks as parts (a) and (c). You should always plan your answers to this type of question before you begin, giving particular attention in your plan to the part worth most marks.

6. The development of tertiary and quaternary activities within a country suggests an advanced economy.
   (a) Explain what is meant by this statement.   (6)
   (b) Using an economic activity you have studied, describe the reasons for its location and the changes which have taken place in recent years.   (12)
   (c) Has the growth of your economic activity been helpful or not to the growth of other economic activities in the area studied?   (7)

Fig. 6.2.2: Section B structured essay question

Essay questions are not divided into parts but simply pose one question to which candidates need to write an essay-style answer that will be marked out of 25 (Fig. 6.2.3 below).

4. The environment has become one of the key political issues of our time. What can the study of geography contribute to this debate?   (25)

Fig. 6.2.3: Section B essay-style question

It is essential that you plan essay answers to avoid losing focus, repeating information and panicking as time starts to run out at the end of the exam. Answers should always relate to the theory that underpins the topic focus and should discuss case studies you have studied. To get the highest marks in this type of question you should attempt, if the question permits, to create an argument and bring into the essay aspects of other thematic topics you have studied. You should ask yourself the following questions before attempting an essay question and keep in mind your answers to these questions when you plan how to answer the question:

- Are the points I am going to make answering the question?
- Do I have plenty of facts and figures relating to at least one case study to back up my answer?
- Am I going to show the examiner my understanding of the theory of the topic on which the question is based?
- Am I going to create an argument within my answer and explain different sides of the argument?
- Am I able to link my answer to this question with other thematic topics?

Essential CASE tip!

Do not choose to do a question in Section B because you prefer the particular style of that question. The most important factor in deciding which question to choose in this section is how well you can answer the question and how well you can express to the examiner your understanding and knowledge of the thematic topic upon which the question is based.

Common mistakes

Timing

Strangely enough, knowing too much information can sometimes be a problem because you simply do not have time to put it down on paper in the exam! You need to learn to be concise, precise and 'mark targeted' when answering any question on the CASE paper to avoid mismanaging your time. This skill comes with practice. It is particularly easy to spend too long answering the question you have chosen in Section A which will then cause you to be under time pressure when choosing and writing your answer in Section B. So keep a close eye on your watch throughout the exam and plan your time as well as what you are going to write.

Essay-style errors

CASE examiners are looking for evidence that the candidate whose paper they are marking has an excellent understanding of Geography. To help show you are such a candidate it is always useful to use the correct geographical terms within a topic.

Both Galore Park Geography textbooks highlight such key terms within the text and explain their meaning in the glossary at the end of each chapter. To help you further, at the end of this chapter you can study the command words Geography CASE examiners use in the exam questions (Appendix 2, page 180) and the syllabus glossary is available for download from www.galorepark.co.uk

When discussing your own opinions within an answer try to avoid using the first person all the time (e.g. I think…). Here are some alternative starting points to use as a tool for expressing your own opinion within an answer:

- It is believed…
- A solution would be…
- One suggests…
- A common view of this…
- This problem could be overcome by…

Repeating information

If you do not read thoroughly and analyse what each part of a layered question is asking, and you do not plan how you are going to respond to each part of the question, it is very easy to find yourself repeating similar or the same information in different parts of the same question. Obviously an examiner cannot give you marks for the same points or information more than once in the exam, so avoid this costly error by quickly planning all parts of all questions before you attempt them.

Identifying your mistakes

The mistakes mentioned so far happen often and are made, to some degree, by all students. However, your teacher will probably give you plenty of past CASE paper questions as practice questions, and you will complete one or two mock CASE papers before doing the real thing in the summer. It is a really good idea to keep all these practice questions and papers and look through them when revising to see if you can identify any of the mistakes discussed above, or any mistake that you have made more than once. Learn from your mistakes and improve your exam technique.

Reading exam questions

Here is some general advice that applies to all parts of the paper. It is advice you have heard before and will hear again, and there is a reason for this! It is absolutely essential that you read the instructions on the front of the paper, know what to do and how long you have to do it. The exam in its present form is one hour long and you have to answer one question from a choice of two in Section A and one question out of a choice of around six questions in Section B. Always read the question carefully, twice to be sure, especially where it is worth several marks. Just as important is to make sure you do answer the question. Look for key words or terms in the question to identify what it wants from you and avoid repeating the same information in different parts of the same question.

Good luck!

Appendix 1: Ordnance Survey map keys

Key taken from 1:25 000 Scale OS Explorer maps

Ordnance Survey®

Explorer™ series (1:25 000 scale)

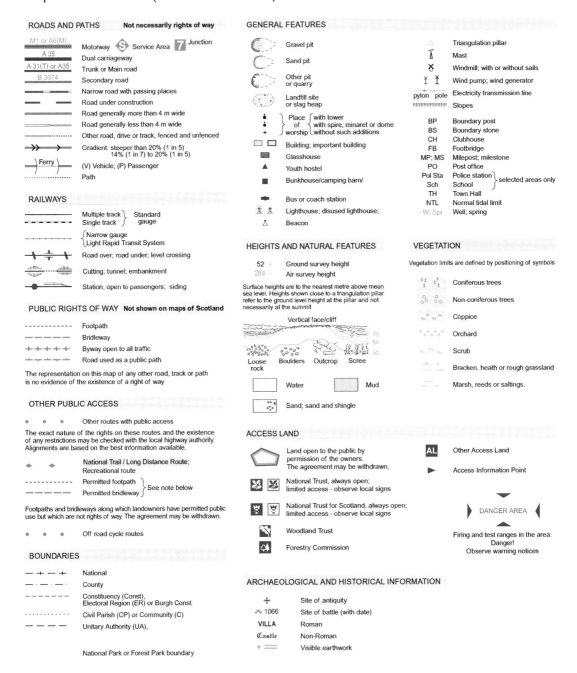

ROADS AND PATHS Not necessarily rights of way

M1 or A6(M)	Motorway Service Area Junction 7
A 35	Dual carriageway
A 31(T) or A35	Trunk or Main road
B 3074	Secondary road
	Narrow road with passing places
	Road under construction
	Road generally more than 4 m wide
	Road generally less than 4 m wide
	Other road, drive or track, fenced and unfenced
	Gradient: steeper than 20% (1 in 5)
	14% (1 in 7) to 20% (1 in 5)
Ferry	(V) Vehicle; (P) Passenger
	Path

RAILWAYS

- Multiple track } Standard gauge
- Single track
- { Narrow gauge
- { Light Rapid Transit System
- Road over; road under; level crossing
- Cutting; tunnel; embankment
- Station, open to passengers; siding

PUBLIC RIGHTS OF WAY Not shown on maps of Scotland

- - - - - - - - Footpath
- — — — — Bridleway
- +++++ Byway open to all traffic
- —·—·—· Road used as a public path

The representation on this map of any other road, track or path is no evidence of the existence of a right of way

OTHER PUBLIC ACCESS

- • • • Other routes with public access

The exact nature of the rights on these routes and the existence of any restrictions may be checked with the local highway authority. Alignments are based on the best information available.

- ◆ ◆ National Trail / Long Distance Route; Recreational route
- - - - - - - Permitted footpath } See note below
- — — — Permitted bridleway

Footpaths and bridleways along which landowners have permitted public use but which are not rights of way. The agreement may be withdrawn.

- • • • Off road cycle routes

BOUNDARIES

- — + — + National
- — · — · — County
- — — — — — Constituency (Const), Electoral Region (ER) or Burgh Const
- · · · · · · · · · Civil Parish (CP) or Community (C)
- — — — — Unitary Authority (UA),

National Park or Forest Park boundary

GENERAL FEATURES

	Gravel pit
	Sand pit
	Other pit or quarry
	Landfill site or slag heap
	Place of worship { with tower { with spire, minaret or dome { without such additions
	Building; important building
	Glasshouse
▲	Youth hostel
■	Bunkhouse/camping barn/
	Bus or coach station
	Lighthouse; disused lighthouse;
	Beacon

△	Triangulation pillar	
	Mast	
✗	Windmill; with or without sails	
	Wind pump; wind generator	
pylon pole	Electricity transmission line	
	Slopes	
BP	Boundary post	
BS	Boundary stone	
CH	Clubhouse	
FB	Footbridge	
MP; MS	Milepost; milestone	
PO	Post office	
Pol Sta	Police station	} selected areas only
Sch	School	
TH	Town Hall	
NTL	Normal tidal limit	
W; Spr	Well; spring	

HEIGHTS AND NATURAL FEATURES

- 52 · Ground survey height
- 284 · Air survey height

Surface heights are to the nearest metre above mean sea level. Heights shown close to a triangulation pillar refer to the ground level height at the pillar and not necessarily at the summit

Vertical face/cliff

Loose rock Boulders Outcrop Scree

- Water
- Mud
- Sand; sand and shingle

ACCESS LAND

	Land open to the public by permission of the owners. The agreement may be withdrawn.
	National Trust, always open; limited access - observe local signs
	National Trust for Scotland, always open; limited access - observe local signs
	Woodland Trust
	Forestry Commission

AL	Other Access Land
►	Access Information Point

DANGER AREA

Firing and test ranges in the area. Danger! Observe warning notices

ARCHAEOLOGICAL AND HISTORICAL INFORMATION

✛	Site of antiquity
✗ 1066	Site of battle (with date)
VILLA	Roman
Castle	Non-Roman
☆	Visible earthwork

VEGETATION

Vegetation limits are defined by positioning of symbols

	Coniferous trees
	Non-coniferous trees
	Coppice
	Orchard
	Scrub
	Bracken, heath or rough grassland
	Marsh, reeds or saltings.

Key taken from 1:25 000 Scale OS Explorer maps (cont.)

 Ordnance Survey®

Explorer™ series (1:25 000 scale)

TOURIST AND LEISURE INFORMATION

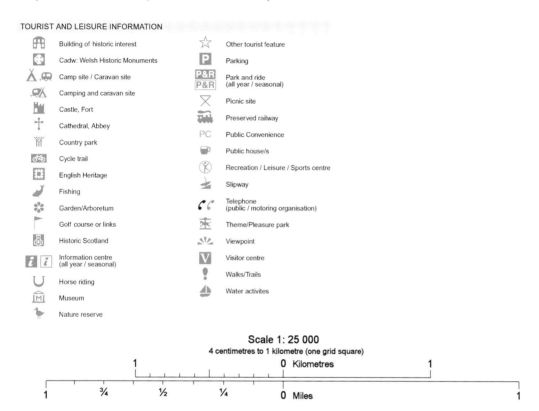

Building of historic interest	Other tourist feature
Cadw: Welsh Historic Monuments	Parking
Camp site / Caravan site	Park and ride (all year / seasonal)
Camping and caravan site	Picnic site
Castle, Fort	Preserved railway
Cathedral, Abbey	Public Convenience
Country park	Public house/s
Cycle trail	Recreation / Leisure / Sports centre
English Heritage	Slipway
Fishing	Telephone (public / motoring organisation)
Garden/Arboretum	Theme/Pleasure park
Golf course or links	Viewpoint
Historic Scotland	Visitor centre
Information centre (all year / seasonal)	Walks/Trails
Horse riding	Water activites
Museum	
Nature reserve	

Scale 1: 25 000
4 centimetres to 1 kilometre (one grid square)

1   0 Kilometres   1

1   ¾   ½   ¼   0 Miles   1

NB. Due to changes in specification there are differences on some sheets

Key taken from 1:50000 Scale OS Landranger maps

Ordnance Survey®

OS Landranger® (1:50 000 scale)

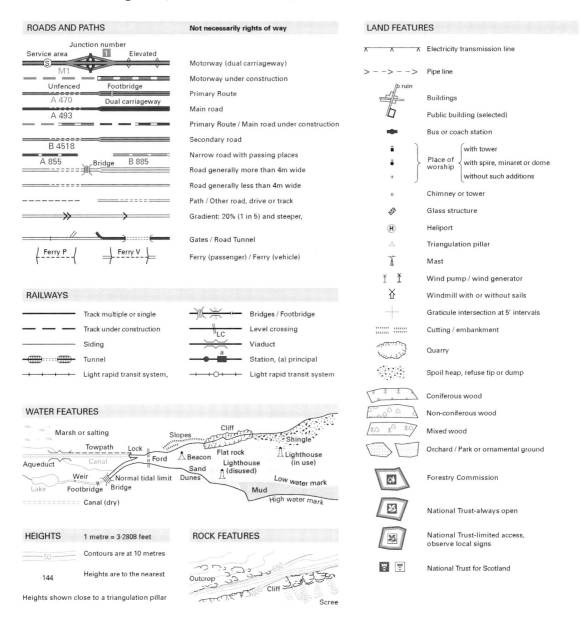

ROADS AND PATHS
Not necessarily rights of way

Junction number
Service area — Elevated
M1

Motorway (dual carriageway)

Motorway under construction

Unfenced — Footbridge
A 470 — Dual carriageway

Primary Route

A 493

Main road

Primary Route / Main road under construction

B 4518

Secondary road

A 855 — Bridge — B 885

Narrow road with passing places

Road generally more than 4m wide

Road generally less than 4m wide

Path / Other road, drive or track

Gradient: 20% (1 in 5) and steeper,

Gates / Road Tunnel

Ferry P — Ferry V

Ferry (passenger) / Ferry (vehicle)

RAILWAYS

Track multiple or single
Track under construction
Siding
Tunnel
Light rapid transit system,

Bridges / Footbridge
Level crossing LC
Viaduct
Station, (a) principal — a
Light rapid transit system

WATER FEATURES

Marsh or salting
Towpath — Lock
Aqueduct — Canal
Weir — Normal tidal limit
Lake — Footbridge — Bridge
Canal (dry)

Slopes — Cliff
Shingle
Flat rock — Lighthouse (in use)
Beacon — Lighthouse (disused)
Sand — Low water mark
Dunes
Mud
High water mark

HEIGHTS
1 metre = 3·2808 feet

— 50 — Contours are at 10 metres

·144 Heights are to the nearest

Heights shown close to a triangulation pillar

ROCK FEATURES

Outcrop
Cliff
Scree

LAND FEATURES

Electricity transmission line

Pipe line

ruin
Buildings
Public building (selected)

Bus or coach station

Place of worship — with tower
with spire, minaret or dome
without such additions

Chimney or tower

Glass structure

(H) Heliport

△ Triangulation pillar

Mast

Wind pump / wind generator

Windmill with or without sails

Graticule intersection at 5' intervals

Cutting / embankment

Quarry

Spoil heap, refuse tip or dump

Coniferous wood

Non-coniferous wood

Mixed wood

Orchard / Park or ornamental ground

Forestry Commission

National Trust-always open

National Trust-limited access, observe local signs

National Trust for Scotland

Key taken from 1:50 000 Scale OS Landranger maps (cont.)

OS Landranger® (1:50 000 scale)

PUBLIC RIGHTS OF WAY

- ················· Footpath
- – – – – – – Bridleway
- –·–·–·–·– Road used as a public path
- –+–+–+–+– Byway open to all traffic

The symbols show the defined route so far as the scale of mapping will allow. Rights of way are not shown on maps of Scotland.

The representation on this map of any other

Danger Area — Firing and Test Ranges in

BOUNDARIES

- –+– –+– –+– National
- –+– –+– –+– District
- –·–·–·– County, Unitary Authority,
- National Park

OTHER PUBLIC ACCESS

- • • • • Other route with public access
- ◆ ◆ National Trail, European Long
- ● ● National/Regional Cycle Network
- — — Surfaced cycle route
- 4 8 National/Regional Cycle Network

ANTIQUITIES

- + Site of monument
- · ○ Stone monument
- ⚔ Battlefield (with date)
- ☆ ···· Visible earthwork
- VILLA Roman
- Castle Non-Roman

TOURIST INFORMATION

- ⋏ Camp site
- 🚐 Caravan site
- ✿ Garden
- ⚑ Golf course or links
- 𝑖 𝑖 Information centre, all year / seasonal
- 🦢 Nature reserve
- P P&R Parking, Park and ride, all year / seasonal
- ✗ Picnic site
- Selected places of tourist interest
- ☎ ☎ Telephone, public / motoring organisation
- ☼ Viewpoint
- Ⓥ Visitor centre
- ! Walks / Trails
- ▲ Youth hostel

ABBREVIATIONS

CG	Coastguard	P	Post office
CH	Club house	PC	Town Hall, Guildhall or equivalent
MP	Milepost	PH	Public house
MS	Milestone		

Scale 1: 50 000
2 centimetres to 1 kilometre (one grid square)

NB. Due to changes in specification there are differences on some sheets

Ordnance Survey, the OS Symbol and OS Landranger are registered trademarks of Ordnance Survey, the national mapping agency of Great Britain. July 2002
Made, printed and published by Ordnance Survey, Southampton, United Kingdom. **For educational use only.** © Crown copyright 2002

Appendix 2: Syllabus command words used in Common Entrance and Common Academic Scholarship papers

annotate – add descriptive explanatory labels

choose – select carefully from a number of alternatives

complete – finish, make whole

define – give an exact description of

describe – write down the nature of the feature

develop – expand upon an idea

explain – write in detail how something has come into being and / or changed

give – show evidence of

identify – find evidence of

list – put a number of examples in sequence

mark and name – show the exact location of and add the name

name – give a precise example of

select – pick out as most suitable or best

shade and name – fill in the area of a feature and add the name

state – express fully and clearly in words

study – look at and / or read carefully

suggest – propose reasons or ideas for something

Scholarship only

discuss – present viewpoints from various aspects of a subject

elaborate – similar to *expand* and *illustrate*

expand – develop an argument and / or present greater detail on

illustrate – use examples to develop an argument or a theme

Index